IMMORTAL MAN

IMMORTAL MAN

A Compilation of Lectures
presented by

Neville

Edited by
Margaret Ruth Broome

DeVorss Publications

ISBN: 0-87516-723-3
Library of Congress Catalog Card Number: 77-81534

First DeVorss Publications Edition, 1999

DeVorss & Company, Publisher
P.O. Box 550
Marina del Rey, CA 90294

Printed in The United States of America

Dedicated to:

Vicki, without whose love
and constant encouragement
physically, mentally, and spiritually,
this book might never have been.

Table of Contents

Foreword

Neville was once described as "a dynamic, handsome and most charming personality. He has a winning smile— thoroughly and completely disarming. His presentation of truth is forceful and sincere. Charged with feeling, and reflecting his own integrity and purposefulness, he communicates himself readily from the pulpit."*

This is true. If you ever heard him speak you might not have agreed with him, in fact you might not have even understood him, but deep within you knew he was speaking the truth.

I attended Neville's lectures the last ten years of his life, and, having recorded them, I have transcribed, edited and compiled a group of twenty-four for this book. Each chapter is a lecture and each lecture is complete within itself.

Neville never "read" his lectures, he never used notes, yet he knew and could quote the Bible verbatim. He had a collection of Bibles that would be the envy of any collector, and spent at least eight hours a day reading them. At times he quoted from the Catholic Bible, the Germanic or the King James, but the one most often used, I have found, is the Revised Standard Version.

*The Romance of Metaphysics, by Israel Regardie

Neville never theorized, never speculated, but spoke only from his own personal experience. Having discovered the truth hidden from the ages, the truth that will set you free, I am sharing it with you as he shared it with me.

Take his message to heart, test yourself, use it daily and make your world your dream come true! You can, you know, for:

"I give you the end of a golden string, Only wind it into a ball: It will lead you in at Heaven's gate, Built in Jerusalem's wall."*

* Wm. Blake, "Jerusalem," plate 77

MARGARET RUTH BROOME

TEST
YOURSELVES

The eternal body of man is the imagination and that is God Himself, the one we speak of in scripture as Jesus Christ. We are told to examine ourselves to see if we are holding to the faith. "Test yourselves," said Paul, "Do you not realize that Jesus Christ is in you? Unless, of course, you fail to meet the test."

You have just had the test and you alone can judge whether you have failed it or not, for you heard the word Jesus Christ and the word God. If it conveyed the sense of an existent something outside of you, you have failed the test. When you hear the words God, Jesus, Christ or Lord and your mind jumps to something outside of YOU (outside of Man), you have failed the test.

We are told, "By Him all things were made and without Him was not anything made that was made." That, I tell you, is your own wonderful human imagination. What is now proved in this world was once only imagined. This is the greatest of all secrets, the secret of imagining. Something that you and I and everyone in the world should strive to understand. For the secret of imagining is the greatest of all problems to the solution of which everyone should aspire, for supreme power, supreme wisdom, supreme delight lies in the solution of this mystery.

When you discover imagination, you discover God, for you have found the creative power of the universe as your own wonderful human imagination. But imagination will do little for our wish until we have imagined the wish fulfilled. As Shakespeare said, "It hath been taught us from the primal state, that which is was wish until it were."

You and I want something. We define our objective. Now, how do we realize it? If this power is within us, then we must learn to operate it. We cannot seek anyone on the outside, for it's within us.

How do I operate it? Let me put it this way. The subjective appropriation of the objective hope is the way to success. It's imagining as if it were true. What would the feeling be like if it were true?

I start from the feeling of the wish fulfilled. I must begin by feeling I have already arrived, already achieved my goal. Then catch the mood that would be mine if it were true and *wear* that mood. If I do, I will realize it in my world.

A friend of mine told me of her recent visit to Pittsburgh. Friends of hers were a little down because of the seeming recession. One friend had worked for twenty-seven years at Jones & Laughlin, one of the large steel firms of our country. He had to put in three more years to complete his thirty years with the firm and retire with a very good retirement fund; but he also had six more years before he could draw his social security, and in the past few months they had laid off over four thousand workers—and it was rumored they were going to close the plant.

The Bible tells us that the depth of our own being speaks to us through the medium of dreams and visions. She took a vision of mine and explained it. Call it a vision if you will, but to me it was just as real as this. I was taken in spirit into an enormous mansion. Three generations were present, but one was invisible; that was the grandfather.

The grandfather, now departed from this world, had

left behind an enormous fortune for the benefit of his son
and his grandchildren. The father said to the children,
"While standing on an empty lot grandfather used to say,
'I remember when this was an empty lot.' Then he would
paint a word picture so vividly of what he intended to do,
it ceased to be an empty lot and you saw the structure he
intended to build. He acted as though it were already a
completed act. He began with the feeling of having arrived
at his ideal for that empty lot."

I awoke on my bed and recalled the dream. I knew the
depths of my own being had constructed that scene to
instruct me. Here is one facet of the great use of this
power called imagination, which is God.

It was too early to rise, so I went back to sleep and
redreamed the dream, but this time I am the grandfather. I
am standing on a vacant lot saying, "I remember when this
was an empty lot."

She reminded him of this technique and said, "You are
afraid you might be let out. I will now remember *when*
you were afraid. I will remember *when* you thought it all
came to an end."

Then he said to her, "Two years ago I was interviewed
for an article in the trade paper and thought it was very
good. But it has never appeared, and I wonder what they
have done with it." She said, "I will read that magazine.
You have told me it is humorously written, so I will take
that magazine in my hand right now and read all about
you."

That was three months ago. Now she tells me, "I have
received the magazine, and in it is a very well written,
humorous article about this man. Also, I heard on the
radio this morning that Jones and Laughlin have decided
not to close the plant, but to spend thirteen million dollars
to modernize it. Then, beginning January 1st, to recall
over four thousand workers they had let out."

Now he is walking on air, but, like most people, he will
still forget it. He will turn to a God outside of himself.
This, as far as he is concerned, would have happened any-

way . . . they would have spent the thirteen million, brought back the four thousand, printed the article seemingly lost for two years . . . and man goes blindly on worshiping a false god because he does not know God.

The ONLY God is your own Wonderful Human Imagination. The only name forever and forever that is HIS name is I AM. "That is my name forever and forever." "When you go to the people of Israel and they ask you, 'What is his name,' tell them 'I AM, that is who I AM and by this name I shall be known throughout all generations.'" There is no other name.

You cannot separate I AM from yourself. That's your essential being. When you say I AM, you are all imagination. You cannot stick imagination on the outside and point to it. You do not observe imagination as you do objects in space, because you are the reality that is called imagination.

You can test it. What would the feeling be like if it were true that I AM now the man I would like to be? Catch the mood, for the mood determines the fortunes of people rather than the fortunes determine the mood. Man puts it just the opposite.

"If I had a million," he will say, "I would feel so good." Now feel as you would if you had it. Catch the mood and the mood will create that ojective hope. What would the feeling be like if you were now the person you want to be? Catch that mood and wear it as you would a suit of clothes, and that mood will create an objective state in your world.

I know from my own experience, it's a mood. I can tell from the mood that possesses me through the day I will meet a certain character, and I do. It may be someone I know, or a total stranger, but I'm drawing into my world an affinity with that mood. You can catch a mood and create a world that is in harmony with it. Anyone can do it; in fact, you are doing it morning, noon and night.

But when you turn to some external god you are turning to a false god. There is no external god. "Examine yourselves," said Paul, "to see whether you are holding to your faith." Test yourselves. Do you not realize that Jesus Christ is in you? Unless, indeed you fail to meet the test.

You have just had the test. If you think of some being on the outside when I use the word Jesus Christ, you have the wrong Jesus Christ, for we are told, "By Him all things were made and without Him was not anything made that is made."

Look around you. All that you see was once only imagined. The suit you wear, your dresses, shoes, everything here; this building was once only conceived in the human imagination, then executed. If all things were made by him, then I must find out who he is, and I can't go beyond my own imagination. He creates all things? Yes, good, bad and indifferent. He waits on me just as quickly and just as indifferently when the will in me is evil as when it is good.

Is that in scripture? Read it in the 32nd chapter of the Book Deuteronomy. "I kill, I make alive, I wound, I heal and none can deliver out of my hand. I, even I am He and beside me there is no other god." I AM is that God.

We are told in the 46th Psalm, "Be still and know that I AM God." Man will not believe it, yet he has evidence morning, noon and night that his own wonderful creative power, which is his own wonderful human imagination, is producing the phenomena of his life. He sees it all around him but shuns it away. It's easier for him to genuflect before some little thing made by the human hand. He will put it on the wall and cross himself for luck and think he has done his duty for the day. He goes to church, sings the hymns with all the others, gives generously to the church and feels he has done his duty. That's all right, if you get any pleasure out of it, do it, but that's not serving the True God.

If you want a social gathering, certainly, go to church. Go to the coffee breaks following the service and ask 100 per cent of those who came out of the service what the text was, and they will give you a vacant look, for they will not know. But it's a place to go on certain days of the year, especially Christmas and Easter, and they think they are doing God a favor.

You are walking with God morning, noon and night. You bring him to bed with you, because your essential being is God and there is no other God. Were He not in you you couldn't even breathe, for your breath is God. Every child born of woman is God incarnate. If man only realized this there would be no wars, for killing man is killing God. Every child born of woman is the incarnation of God, whether he be black, yellow, pink, white or any other color.

The story as told us in scripture is true, but not as it's told. The day will come you will find yourself re-enacting the entire drama as told us in the gospel, and you will know who he is in a first person singular, present tense experience. He comes to us as one unknown, yet one who in the most wonderful, mysterious manner lets man experience who he is. When you experience who He is, you are He.

In the meantime when you dream of some wonderful objective in this world that is not yet realized, remember who the dreamer is . . . the dreamer is God and God is your own Wonderful Human Imagination. Do not let your reason and your senses dictate what is possible. All things are possible to God. If you are going to accept the facts of life and let reason dictate it, you'll never go beyond where you are. Suspend them just for a moment and try this technique.

What would the feeling be like? How would I feel if it were true that I am already the man I would like to be? How would my friends see me? Bring them into your mind's eye and let them see you, talk to you and congratulate you on your good fortune. Don't duck, accept the congratulations of your friends. Actually play the part all within yourself and then believe it 100 per cent.

We are told in John's letter, the 5th chapter, the 15th verse of his 1st Epistle: "If we believe that He hears us in all that we ask of Him, then we know we have obtained the request made of Him." If you get the right God you have no doubts in your mind as to whether He heard you or not, for you know you heard it and that's God. Maybe you do not think you are good enough, but you can't deny you hear your own mind. You hear your own inner conversations; you hear your own inner speech, and, if you know *that* one is God, then you are sure He heard you.

Let me repeat, "If we know that He hears us in all that we ask of Him, then we know we have already obtained the request made of Him." All right, there is an interval between that imaginal act and its fulfillment, as there is between the creative act of a man and the birth of his child. Everything has an interval of time between the act and its fulfillment.

A horse will take 11 months, a woman 9, a little sheep 5, a chicken 21 days. There are always intervals of time, so the Bible teaches. "Every vision has its own appointed hour; it ripens, it will flower. If it be long, wait, for it is sure and it will not be late."

Find who He is, for he is a living God, not a dead God. Read the 115th Psalm about the kind of gods men worship. The whole psalm is devoted to the false god that the whole vast world worships. "They have mouths but speak not; eyes but see not; ears but hear not, hands but feel not; feet but walk not." Just a dead thing made by human hands; when the living God within man has his own wonderful human imagination.

"All that you behold, though it appears without, it is within in your own womderful human imagination, of which this world of mortality is but a shadow." All things exist in the human imagination. Everything you see as an objective reality was produced by imagining.

You can't think of one thing that would deny it. Go to the moon? You first had to imagine it. You had to imagine everything concerning the machine that took you to the moon. Everything in the world first has to be imagined and then executed. Take the blueprint first, conceive it and dwell in it as though it were true, and no power on earth can stop it from becoming so.

Prayer is nothing more than the subjective appropriation of the objective hope. That is the way to success. I appropriate it subjectively.

Suppose you wanted a ball, an ordinary baseball, but one was not available. Assume you are holding a baseball in your hand until you can feel it. To prove to yourself you have held the baseball, assume you are now holding a tennis ball. Do you feel the difference? Now a golf ball, a piece of silk, do you feel any difference? If you can distinguish between these many objects, although they are subjective, they must exist somewhere.

Can you smell a rose? A rose has an odor all of its own. Now can you smell an Easter lily? What does this mean? You are going to get them. Someone will think of you and send you flowers, and they will be the flowers you felt, touched and smelled, for it works that way.

Money has an odor unlike any other in the world. It's more fragrant to the miser than the most marvelous perfume. Put a money bag to a miser's nose and it's like putting roses to mine, he loves it so. Put a twenty dollar bill in your hand; feel it; then a piece of paper. You can tell the difference in touch and odor.

All this is part of the inner man and all things are possible to him. Before you condemn it, try it. Then, if you have the evidence to support my claim, it doesn't matter what the world will tell you. If they laugh at you, so what? They laughed at the idea of going to the moon and now it is an accomplished fact. There are still those who won't believe it happened because they don't want to believe it. There are those who said you couldn't live under water, but we have the submarine.

But try it first. If it proves itself in performance, then it doesn't really matter what the whole vast world thinks. Go about your Father's business (which is yourself) and live a full and wonderful life in this world of Caesar. Then the day will come and you will depart this age. Those who are departing it now, unless they are awakened, will still find themselves in a world just like this.

But those who have awakened and experienced the second birth, the birth from above, will find themselves in an entirely different age, where they are all imagination and wherever they go everything is perfect, for all things must conform to them and they are perfect. That's heaven.

Heaven is not an area; it's not a realm; it's a body. When that body is awakened within you, which is your wonderful human imagination completely awake, wherever you go clothed in that body everything is perfect. If you found yourself in a forest of dead trees, they would all burst into foliage. The desert would bloom like the rose because you are there. No blind, deaf, or handicapped man could stand in your presence but would be instantly transformed into a perfect man because you are perfect. That's heaven; it's harmony. It's not a place where you are going to go, pearly streets and all that nonsense, no it's *you* in a world that is perfect because you are perfect.

The day will come when you will awaken that body. It is in you but it's sound asleep. One day you will know the mystery of the resurrection when you rise within yourself, for the only grave in which the Lord is buried is your own skull. That's His tomb, and one day He will awake and it's you who will come out of that tomb. Then you will know who you are.

He is buried in every child in the world . . . this universal being, yet one. Billions of us, yet only one Lord, and that one Lord in his Fullness is buried in you individually and when you awaken you are He.

Take a goal, make it a lovely goal either for yourself or for another. For any time you exercise your imagination lovingly on behalf of another you are mediating God to that other. Bring a friend before your mind's eye. Represent him to yourself as the man, as the woman you would like him to be. Don't tell them, ask for no praise, just assume they are talking to you and telling you the most

marvelous news about themselves. Congratulate them on
that news and go your own way. Believe in the reality of
that imaginal act. It may happen tomorrow, the day after,
a week or a month later, but it has its own appointed hour;
it ripens and it will flower. Don't be concerned, just leave
it alone and it will come to pass.

We are always imagining ahead of our evidence, so go
to the end and feel it. Dwell in that end even though
reason denies it and your senses deny it. Turn your back
upon the doubters, which are your senses, your reason, for
that's hell or the devil or satan in this world. Turn your
back and walk as though things were as you want them to
be. Live in that assumption and it will slowly harden into
fact, even though at the moment of your assumption it is
denied by reason. An assumption, though false, if persisted
in will harden into fact. Learn to assume and persist in the
assumption and it will come to pass.

Before you throw it away, try it; just try it. I am not
telling you it is easy to outgrow fixed ideas concerning
God. I confess that when I experienced it, it was an awful
shock to me, for I was raised in a wonderful Christian
environment and firmly believed what I was told. I still call
myself a Christian but not an orthodox Christian, for I
have found him, him of whom Moses and the law and the
prophets wrote. They were writing all about me. The day
will come you are going to find him, and you, too, will
know who thay wrote about, for you are going to find
Him as yourself.

DIVINE BREAKTHROUGHS

The Bible is a record of divine breakthroughs, revealing God's plan of redemption. But it is a riddle, a parable.

We turn to the 78th Psalm. The writer tells us to listen carefully, for he is going to speak in a parable. A parable is a story told as if it were true, leaving the one who hears it to discover its fictitious character and learn its lesson. It's a story with a message.

He tells us it is a riddle of things past. Things our fathers told their children to tell to coming generations. Then he takes the entire history of Israel as recorded in Book of Exodus and repeats it. He tells of the great wonders God performed as He led Israel from bondage to freedom, yet Israel turned away from Him constantly. Then, in the end, God awoke as a man awakes from sleep and He chose David. He took him from the sheep and made him shepherd of His people Jacob. David led them wisely, with a diligent heart, and brought them to the Lord.

The whole story is all about you. The drama as told in scripture is the drama of a father and a son. The father is God. His name is I AM. His son is David.

I know this is a bold statement to make to those who have been trained in some other concept, but I am not theorizing; I'm not speculating; I am speaking from experience.

Our teachers have substituted their concepts and their speculation for vision. We are told, "Where there is no vision the people cast off all restraint." They let go. Men who call themselves teachers (self-appointed teachers) are men without vision, and they have completely changed the entire picture.

They speak of Jesus as a man, as something on the outside. No, Jesus is the Lord. He is a father and his son is David. That son is the Messiah, the one who is anointed. "I have anointed him with my holy oil."

It's a drama between the father and the son. The son can say, "I and my father are one, but my father is greater than I." For in the office of the sent, he is inferior to his essential being as the sender, but they are one.

We are told, "No one can say Jesus is Lord except by the Holy Spirit." The Holy Spirit is the Remembrancer. Man awakes and begins to remember.

The Lord and his son are placed in man as told us in Ecclesiastes, "God has put eternity into man's mind yet so that man cannot find out what he has done from the beginning to the end." In the end you will know what He has done, for everything you have ever done is the will of the Father. In the end you awake and your son David reveals you as God the Father. That is the drama.

We are told, "He has granted unto us His precious and very great promises, that through these we may escape from the corruption that is in the world and partake of His divine nature."

What are the promises? That when I awake I am He. No one in the world can convince me I am He but his son who calls me Father. When He stands before you, you know you are looking at your son David of Biblical fame. That is the Christ. That is the son of God.

In scripture Jesus is the Lord, for David in the spirit calls Him My Lord, a title always referred to by the son when he speaks of his father. If David called Him My Lord, how can He be David's son? He is David's father.

It has happened to me. It comes at the end. "Lord, show me my end." I'll show you the end when the end arrives. When it arrives you will know, for there will be no more restoration for you. Resurrection is yours, for resurrection is the entrance door into the new age.

I do not accept reincarnation as the world teaches it. Scripture does not teach reincarnation. It does teach a second birth, which is resurrection. You are now sound asleep in a tomb called Golgotha in scripture or, in the Book of Luke, it is translated skull.

It's the Lord who is buried in the skull of man. He is dreaming a dream and the dream does not terminate when you die. You are restored to life in a world just like this (terrestrial); but you are about twenty years old and you continue the journey.

Scripture teaches, "Those who are of this age marry and are given in marriage, but those who are accounted worthy to attain to that age, they neither marry nor are they given in marriage, for they cannot die any more, for they are now sons of the resurrection."

He speaks of marriage belonging to this age, and this age does not terminate when someone dies, he is still in this age. The world is just like this; it's real; it's solid. It's not made of gossamer. A man is restored to life and goes on and on with the same identity.

As far as I am concerned I am individualized. You are individualized and we tend forever toward even greater and greater individualization, but not reincarnation. It would be a horrible monstrosity if the individual ceases to be individual. What would he be? Nothing.

I know that millions of people in the world teach reincarnation and believe it, and do all kinds of things on the outside to perpetuate it. I know of one chap who is a handsome East Indian. He put out a book showing himself as a woman, a man, a Chinese, and Indian, all of these claiming these were pictures of his reincarnations, male and female. Years later, when he matured and could repute it, he publicly denied it, but the book was already printed and thousands of copies sold. You can still find it in our libraries.

He will die one day (he is in his seventies now), but the book will remain. And in the tomorrows men will say, "Here is one who knew it." Yet he denied it completely after the damage was done.

Reincarnation does not in any way answer the problem. You are individualized and you tend forever and forever towards even greater individualization. To tell me I am suffering today because of what I have done, how many unnumbered millenniums would Stalin have to live for taking the lives of twenty million innocent people? How many millenniums would Hitler have to suffer for taking six million innocent Jews and putting them in furnaces, plus what he did with his air power?

No, God is merciful. It's a nightmare. No reincarnation. This play goes on and on and on. You cannot awaken as God without the furnaces, and these are the furnaces. He uses all things for good. We intended it for evil but He intended it for good, and in the end He is going to bring it out—for good.

All these things around us don't really change. We think they are changing because we now fly to the moon, take a jet to New York in three hours instead of months in some wagon, but things haven't changed. We are told in Ecclesiastes, "What has been is what will be and what has been done is what will be done and there is nothing new under the sun."

Almost sixty years ago we had the revolution that Marx and Lenin created, and the very state they said would wither away has become stronger and stronger. In the name of freedom, freedom was taken away. What they thought they would supplant has been reinforced. It's called a new name now, the USSR, but with impunity Stalin murdered twenty million people. No czar has that record. So what did they change? They didn't change a thing.

This is the world in which we live and we remain in

it until the very end. The end will justify all the horrors you and I have gone through, for He has placed within us Himself and his son. The son is doing the Father's will.

We are put through the furnaces of affliction for whose sake? "For my own sake," said he, "I will not give my glory to another. His glory is Himself." He finally breaks down the bar of perdition between you and Himself and you become God.

We are destined to awake one day as God. There is no other being in the world but the Lord. You will not be called Jesus, but you will know you are the father of his son. If you are the father of his son, then you are Jesus. "No one can say Jesus is the Lord except by the Holy Spirit," by rememberance. For the moment you see Him, memory returns, and you have always been the Father of David, and He has always been your son.

He's not an old man, he's eternally young. You can't describe the beauty of David. No artist could paint him. No one could sculpture him. He is described in the Book of Samuel as ruddy with beautiful eyes and fair of complexion. That's what he is and you know exactly who you are when you look at him.

These are breakthroughs revealing God's plan of redemption. Everyone is going to experience it, for He is the shepherd. While we are here we are the fragmented being. We are told, "I say you are gods, sons of the most high all of you; nevertheless you will die like men and fall as one man among princes."

God Himself entered death's door and actually laid down in the grave with me in my own wonderful skull. That's where He dreams and He has a nightmare, a daymare. But in the end God awakes as from sleep and calls David from the flocks—and appoints him shepherd of his people Jacob. He shepherds them wisely and singleheartedly and brings them to the Father.

Read the 78th Psalm. It's good to read it in many Bibles. Read it in the King James, Revised Standard and even the New English Bible. They change it somewhat; it

doesn't have the poetry of the King James but it's beautifully done.

These breakthroughs come only through vision. You
cannot speculate and arrive at anything concerning scripture. Scripture is revealed truth which cannot be logically
proven. As you are told in that Psalm, "I will give you the
riddle of the past." Then He tells you the stories of how
He led them out of Egypt; how He parted the water;
brought manna out of the nowhere and yet they turned
away. Then, in the very end, the Lord awoke as from
sleep.

This great mystery is all within you. The whole vast
world is yourself pushed out. You are living in a world of
your own dream. "All that you behold, though it appears
without, it is within in your own wonderful human imagination, of which this world of mortality is but a shadow."

I have experienced these breakthroughs. It's a series of
the most wonderful supernatural experiences. They come
at stated intervals, taking a period of 1260 days to complete that which is foretold in scripture. The Old Testament is adumbrated; it's a foreshadowing in a not altogether conclusive or immediately evident way. The New
Testament gives meaning to it, but man has misunderstood
the meaning and worships something he himself created—
and puts it on the outside.

The whole thing unfolds within man. "He has put
eternity into the mind of man yet so that man cannot find
out what he has done from the beginning to the end."
What did he do? He put Himself and his son into your
mind, and He is dreaming the dream of life with you. In
the end you will awaken and you are God, the very God
that creates and sustains the heavens.

Not a little God, but the Only God. "Hear O Israel, the
Lord, our God, the Lord is One," not two. There can only
be one and that's the one you are. In the end you will be
the father of my son, therefore you and I are one.

"I have found in David a man after my own heart who
will do all my will." Who was his father? He said he was

the son of Jesse. The word Jesse means, "Jehovah exists."
It's any form of the verb "to be." His name forever is I Am
and Jesse is I AM.

When David stands before you, who is his father? I
AM. He will stand before you and you know you are his
father, so you are saying "I AM," and that's God's name
forever and forever.

Now this may not sit well with you, but I would not
retract one word because I have experienced scripture. The
whole thing has unfolded itself within me. The end comes
only when David appears. Then the dove descends and the
seal of approval is placed upon you, for the journey is over;
you have returned as the victor, for you have awakened
the Father who slept and dreamed the dream of life.

We all must dream as our forefathers did. But if we
know the principle upon which his law rests, we can
cushion some of the inevitable blows. When you know
what you want, assume the feeling of the wish fulfilled and
persist in that assumption. Though your senses and your
reason deny the reality of the assumption, if you persist in
it, it will harden into fact. You begin by feeling you have
already arrived at the end.

What would the feeling be like if you were the man
you want to be? Assume you are that man. Everything
may deny it, but, if you persist in assuming you are already the man you want to be, you will become it.

You are all imagination. Blake said it so beautifully in
his *Jerusalem,* "Babel mocks saying there is no God or son
of God. That thou, O human imagination, are all a delusion. But I know thee O Lord. When thou ariseth upon my
weary eyes even in this iron mill. You also suffer with me
although I behold you not. Then the divine voice answered,
Fear not, I am with you always. Only believe in me that I
have power to raise from death your brother who sleeps in
Albion." We are all asleep in the one man, Albion. Believe
in this power, which he calls the Lord, which is your own
wonderful human imagination.

But to try to change the circumstances of life before

you change your imaginal activity is to struggle against the very nature of things. For these things are but the results of your imaginings. If you don't change it you cannot change the fruit it bears.

Everyone is free to imagine, for the God who created the universe and sustains it is within you. When you say, "I am," that's He. His son as His creative power and His wisdom is there, too. In the 11th chapter of Revelations we read, "The kingdoms of the world have become the kingdom of our Lord and of His Christ." Jesus is the Lord and His Son is Christ. But in the office of the Christ he is doing the will of the Father (the dreamer in man); but in the end He is one with the Father and can say, "I and my Father are one."

Then when you take off this garment you are the Lord reunited into one being who is God. Then a new venture—and who knows what that will be? All must return; not one will be lost. Not one in eternity can be lost. When all are gathered into the one being, then we will plot another adventure, for God is forever and expanding. It would be horrible, after this wonderful adventure, no matter how glorious we are at the end of it, to simply bask in that glory. No, we are creative beings and we have to expand, so we will conceive something more difficult and venture again.

I can't conceive of stopping at a certain point. Arrive at a certain goal and then be satisfied? That's not creativity. I'm all for the creative spirit. Can you imagine an Einstein wanting to stop because he discovered that wonderful principle of his? No, he only scratched the surface. We go on expanding and expanding and expanding forever. God is infinite and you are that God.

We are all asking questions about the next world and we are still lost in this one. Tennyson said it so beautifully in "The Poem." "Be patient, our playwright will show in some fifth act what this wild drama means." When the curtain comes down on the end, we will be drawn into the conference and then another plot. I'm all for it!

For this whole vast world is only a theater to express the power and wisdom of the author of it all, and the author is in man. When you say, "I AM," that sense of awareness is God. You are the Lord, and you are dreaming this dream of life. Your son David is executing your every dream. He never wavers. Whether you dream noble dreams or ignoble dreams David will do it. In the end David will unveil you as his father, and you will know you are the Lord and David is your son.

IMAGINATION
The Basis of All That Is !

Jesus said, "Think not that I have come to abolish the law and the prophets. I am come not to abolish them but to fulfill them." The one speaking is now present within you. When he awakes you will hear these words and you will find them to be YOUR words. That one is your own wonderful *human* imagination. That one is God.

Imagination is the basis of all that is. What is now proved to be true as far as we are concerned was once only imagined. Think of something in the world that is to you real, that wasn't first imagined. The secret of imagining is the secret of God. The secret of imagining is the greatest of all problems to the solution of which every one should aspire, because supreme power, supreme wisdom, supreme delight lie in the far-off solution of this mystery. I can acquaint you with it and then leave you to your choice and its risk, because everything in the world is created by this power. He said, "I kill and I make alive. I wound and I heal and none can deliver out of my hand. I create the light and make darkness. I create woe and I make weal, and I, even I am He, and there is no other God beside me." That's your own wonderful human imagination.

There are secrets to this power and you and I, by experiment, try to discover the secret. As we discover the secret of imagining, we are discovering the secret of God.

God and the Human Imagination are synonymous terms, they are interchangeable. We read that, "If we know that He hears us in whatever we ask of Him, we know we have already obtained that which we requested of Him." No restraint!

You may sit down and commune with what you may think to be other than yourself, but because there are billions of us in the world and only one God, you might wonder if He heard you. But if you identify God with your own wonderful human imagination, you have no doubt in your mind that He heard you.

Can you believe that your own Wonderful Human Imagination is God? We are told in the 4th Psalm, "Commune with your own heart upon your bed and be silent." He hears you if you commune with yourself, but can you believe that to commune with self is to commune with God? If you assume you are the one you would like to be, can you believe God has already answered your prayer?

I do not expect, after a certain conception, that the child will be born tomorrow. The vision has its own appointed hour, it ripens, it will flower. If it be long, then wait, it is sure and it will not be late. A little child takes 9 months, a lamb 5 months, a chicken 21 days, an elephant a year or more. But every conception has its own appointed hour; it ripens and it will flower. If, to you it seems long, wait, for it is sure and it will not be late relative to its own nature.

Dare to assume you are exactly *what* you want to be. Dare to assume you are *where* you want to be even though your reason and your senses deny it. If you do, will it work? It doesn't cost you a penny to try it. You are told, "Come buy wine, buy milk without money." Try it. Try to prove me wrong.

When I didn't have a nickel and desired a trip that would cost me well in excess of $1000, I dared to assume I was there and viewed the world *from* that assumption. Instead of thinking OF it, I thought FROM it. When I thought of where I was physically, in my imagination it was two thousand miles to the northwest of me. Then I slept in that assumption, and in a way I did not consciously devise, it unfolded and that assumption hardened into fact.

We are told, "Blessed is the man who delights in the law of the Lord. In all that he does he prospers." It doesn't say, "If it is good for you." You could choose something that may be horrible, but He tells you your imaginal acts are facts.

"You have heard it said of old you shall not commit adultery, but I say to you any man who looks lustfully upon a woman has already committed the act with her in his heart." He tells us that the restraint of an impulse is not enough, the act was committed at the moment it was imagined. You may contemplate the consequences and be afraid and therefore not complete the act, physically, but your imaginal act was the fact.

No one can stop you from imagining you are secure, but you could say, "I have no money. I am beyond the age of employment; I don't have a rich relative who will leave me anything," and give yourself a thousand reasons why you are not secure, but can you imagine? Who can stop you from imagining? Can you dare imagine you are what you want to be? I can. I have done it unnumbered times. I have done it successfully for those I love dearly as well as those I do not know. I have failed often, too, but the failure is in me and not in the law.

Imagination plus faith is the stuff out of which we make our world. We are told all things are made in this manner. "He calls a thing that is not seen as though it were seen and the unseen becomes seen." When I come to Him I must believe He exists and that He rewards those who believe in Him. I must have faith in the imaginal act.

If I quietly imagine a state, believing I am in communion with God and that my imaginal act is God's act, the results will follow me, for that imaginal act was causal the moment I did it. When it appears in my world I may try to trace the effect to some physical cause and give all credit to it, but I tell you every physical effect has an imaginal cause and not a physical. A physical only seems to be, it is a delusion of our fading memory, for we do not remember when we imagined it.

The other day my dentist said quite innocently to me, "When I saw your mouth and repaired this tooth, I said to myself, 'This tooth will last thirteen years.'" It WAS thirteen years. Had he only said twenty-five, but he didn't, so thirteen years later out came that anchor tooth and therefore complete restructure of my entire mouth. He set it in motion. He didn't tell me, he didn't have to tell me it was HIS imaginal act. I was only the victim of his creative power.

Don't take anything lightly. You are creating morning, noon and night. Your imaginal acts are God's acts because your imagination is God. God actually became as you are that you may become God. He said, "I have tried you in the furnaces of affliction; for my own sake I do it, for my own sake, for how should my name be profaned, my glory I will not give to another."

God's glory is the gift of God Himself as told us in the 33rd chapter of the Book of Exodus. "I will make my glory to pass before you and when I pass by . . ." Glory is equated with the "A" of God, for his name is "I AM" and He cannot give His glory (which is himself) to another.

In becoming man He puts man through the furnaces. If you read the story carefully you will see that He took upon himself all of your infirmities and bore your diseases. Who suffers? You may say, "I am suffering." That's God. "But I'm feeling it, He isn't." There is no He, His name is I AM. I feel the pain, I feel the infirmities, I feel the disease . . . that's God.

"The fool says in his heart there is no God or son of God, that thou, O human imagination, art all a delusion. But I know thee, O Lord, when thou ariseth upon my weary eyes even in this dungeon and this iron mill. Thou also suffer with me although I behold thee not." Then the voice replies, "Fear not, I am with you always."

Can you ever get away from imagining? If you fall asleep now and start dreaming, who is dreaming but imagination. When you awake He is still with you, because you are still imagining, for I AM the reality named imagination.

He promised He would give Himself to you as though there were no other, because in giving Himself to you there is no other. Everything in the world is yourself pushed out and you manipulate it by your imaginal acts.

The day will come you will rise within yourself. You rise from your own skull, for that's the only tomb in the world where God is buried. When you rise you are born, "Born not of blood nor of the will of the flesh (the will of man), but of God." In other words, you are self-begotten.

God begets Himself in you, as told us in the epistle to the Hebrews, "He is bringing many sons to glory." But the sons are numbered; each child born of woman is that son of God as told us in the 32nd chapter of Deuteronomy, "He has set bounds to the people of earth according to the number of the sons of God."

"But," you may say, "There are three billion people in the world." So what? "I will make them more numerous than the stars, more numerous than the sands of the beach." Count them. You can't count the stars, but in scripture the second son is represented by this fabulous number.

The second son went amuck and spent his power unwisely; then coming to his senses he returned to his father, who embraced him and gave him the authority of himself. He gave him the ring, the robe and the fatted calf; in fact everything was given to the one who went out from and then returned to the Father. His gift is the gift of Himself to you, the second son, who came out. "I chose you, in me, before the foundation of the world."

Let the first son complain. He will complain and complain, "I served you and you gave me nothing. Then he said, "My son, all that I have is yours." The most fabulous possession in the world is without meaning unless there is a knowledge of it and a readiness to use it. Unless we went out into the world and misused our imagination as we have done, we could not become aware it is our creative power.

I saw it so clearly one night. I am in a fabulous field of sunflowers. Each sunflower was a human face, but they were all anchored in the earth. They moved in unison, like an orchestra. If one smiled, they all smiled. If one bent over, they all bent over and every one did what the whole did. I didn't see one lead them; they all seemed to do it automatically. And I felt I was freer (limited as I am) than all of them put together, beautiful as they were, but they had not gone out.

I was once part of that infinite garden, totally unaware of what I possessed, and my father chose me in him before the foundation of the world, that I may become aware of my possessions. Having gone through the furnaces of affliction, He wakes within me and then I know who I am.

In the beginning He set up a pattern, and Christ, the pattern man, is buried in you. When this pattern unfolds itself in you, it unfolds as you, and then you know you are the Lord spoken of in scripture as God the Father.

And, like my dentist, you are a creator. He set the whole thing in motion the day he said to himself "It will last thirteen years." I checked it; it was thirteen years.

Blake said in his wonderful *Jerusalem*, "O what have I said, what have I done, O all powerful human words?" For the Word of man is the Word of God, and "My Word shall not return unto me void, it must accomplish that which I purposed and prosper in the thing for which I sent it."

Man forgets his word, and, when it happens, he looks for a physical cause. No one thinks of that moment when the Word went out. For the Word goes forward and It cannot return unto me void; It must accomplish that which I purposed and prosper in the thing for which I sent It.

I can see my father now, back in 1919. He was a ship's chandler. The ships were bringing the boys back from the first world war and the captains would tell him all kinds of stories. At dinner he would say to my mother, "We have

another war in twenty years. It will be against Germany
and Japan." (He didn't mention Italy). "We will again have
America and France as our allies." On the 1st day of
September, 1939, war broke out . . . exactly twenty years
later. My father only repeated what he had heard, but they
were his words and he believed them.

Our headlines, day after day, are setting the picture in
motion for tomorrow's confusion. There are men paid to
write scare headlines. They think it helps sell papers and
isn't going to hurt anyone. It isn't? We are going to fulfill
them. We fulfill all our words because God and man are
one. Man is all imagination, and God is man and exists in
us and we in Him. The eternal body of man is the imagination and that is God himself. God's word is man's word,
and it cannot return unto him void if he speaks it with
conviction.

Imagination, plus faith, these are the very stuff out of
which we fashion our world. Can you commune with yourself and be confident he heard you? You know you heard
yourself. In the 1st epistle of John, the 5th chapter, the
15th verse, we read: "If we know that He hears us in
whatever we ask of Him, we know we have obtained that
which we request of Him." We have already obtained it. It
may appear tonight, depending upon what seed you planted. One seed will grow overnight while other seeds take a
little longer, but each has its own appointed hour. You
want to be wealthy, healthy, happy; no matter what you
want, everything is possible.

I tell you, your own wonderful human imagination is
immortal. That's the man in you that cannot die, for nothing dies; everything is restored. But the day will come you
will go beyond restoration and you will resurrect. In the
meantime do not fail to apply the law. "Blessed is the man
who delights in the law of the Lord; in all that he does, he
prospers." Name your desire and view the world *from* that
assumption, instead of thinking *of* it, and you will manifest it in this world.

Man, being all imagination, must be wherever he is in

his imagination. If, right now, you are seated in a chair and you decide to be elsewhere, you can tell if you have moved by a frame of reference. If you have moved, what do you see? If, in your mind's eye you are still seeing the room, you have not moved, for motion can be detected only by a change of position relative to another object. If you are else, think of your room. If you see it differently you have moved.

Let me tell you a story of a friend of mine. Her name is possibly the most popular in America, the name is Roosevelt. She was of the Teddy Roosevelt branch. In spite of her name she did not have a personal fortune. She came to see me one day and said, "Neville, I am desperate. Unless I rent my home in New York City, we cannot afford to open our place in Long Island." I said, "All right, tonight sleep in your home in Long Island." "But," she said, "How can I go to sleep there?" I said, "You don't do it physically. Physically sleep in your apartment in New York City, but in your imagination sleep in your home in Long Island and think of your place in New York which is rented." "I'll do it, " she said, "and if it rents I'll call you." I said, "There's no 'if' about it, the only 'if' is if you do it, then you'll call me."

The next morning Mrs. Roosevelt called and this is what she said: "I am calling you from Long Island where I slept *physically* last night. I went directly home from your place, and soon after I arrived an agent called, asking to show the apartment. A single man came in, liked it, money meant nothing to him, but he wanted immediate possession; so I called my husband at the office and we moved out last night."

Once she came to see me about her son. He had come back from Egypt with a huge beard. She said, "Neville, I am so embarrassed. I don't want to be seen with him. What must I do, because he gets annoyed and will do nothing his father and I suggest." I said, "How would you feel if you kissed him and he had no beard? You would kiss your son, wouldn't you? Then put your hand on his face and kiss him. Feel his smooth skin, knowing he has no beard." "All right," she said, "I will do that."

I opened the paper one morning to see the picture of a big fashionable wedding. Mrs. Roosevelt, her husband, her son and his bride were coming down the steps of the Episcopal church, and he had no beard!

The next time she came to see me I reminded her and she said, "You know why?" I said, "Yes, I know why, but you tell me." "Well, the girl he married refused to go through with it unless he shaved."

She saw the physical act and it wasn't so at all. There is no natural effect with a natural cause. Every natural effect has an imaginal cause, the natural only seems, but it is a delusion.

I ask you to please take it seriously. Watch your every imaginal act and don't take anything lightly. Don't voice an opinion that may be embarrassing or hurtful to yourself or anyone even though reason dictates it, for your words are the words of God. "O what have I said, what have I done, O all powerful human words?"

ENDS
Ultimate and Temporary

I think you will find this an interesting lecture, for we are taking ends, the ultimate end and then the temporary end, for it is the end that gives meaning to all that goes before.

The Psalmist said, "Lord, let me know my end and the number of my days." Then you read, "Fear not, for it is your Father's *good* pleasure to give you the kingdom of heaven." That's the ultimate end. In giving you the kingdom of heaven He gives you Himself for you can equate heaven with God.

God is able to give Himself to all of us. The gift comes suddenly and without warning after the tribulation of human experience. He said, "I have tried you in the furnaces of afflication for my own sake; for my own sake I do it, for how should my name be profaned? My glory I will not give to another."

When we read the story in the Book of Exodus, we see that glory and God are equated. "I will make my glory to pass before you, and when I pass by . . ." So the "I" and glory are synonymous. He cannot give himself to another.

The furnaces are simply to change man into Himself. He became as I am that I may be as He is. I pass through the tribulation of human experience, then the end comes suddenly. The event comes in unique and unpredictable ways. Man thinks he can discover the way without having experienced it. He can't do it.

Listen to the words carefully now. These are taken from the 48th chapter of Isaiah, the 3rd verse. "The former things I declared of old, they went forth from my mouth and I make them known; then suddenly I did them and they came to pass." Now, the one proclaiming what is going to be done had to fulfill it himself.

If he would give me himself, he has to fulfill it *in* me. When this unpredictable, unique event takes place, it takes place in the first person, singular tense, *in* me. It comes suddenly, without warning. When I actually experience the gift of God to me, it isn't someone on the outside giving me something; He rises within me and then I know who I am.

I have heard preachers claim they have met Jesus and are waiting for him to return. Ask them, "Who is Jesus?" and they will reply, "Jesus is the son of God." Then say to them, "If you met him and say he is the son of God, then you must be God." They will be shocked and think you are blaspheming, yet we are told, "No one knows the son except the father." If they met him and claim he is the son, then they must be God the Father.

I can tell you, you can say right to their face, "You are a liar, because you cannot meet him from without." When you know God, you know him through his son. You aren't going to know him through Jesus, for Jesus is the Father and David is the son. When you meet David you know he is your son, and, because he is God's son, then you know who you are. There is no other way to know God. It's the *only* way. The entire story of scripture comes in unique and unpredictable ways.

"The former things I declared of old. They went forth from my mouth and I made them unknown. Then suddenly I acted and they came to pass." Read it in the 48th chapter of Isaiah.

The word "Isaiah" means "Jehovah saves." It's the

same meaning as the word Jesus or Jehovah. Jehovah is salvation. Jesus means, Jehovah is salvation. The word Jesus and Jehovah are interchangeable terms. "No one can say Jesus is Lord except by the Holy Spirit." Who is the Holy Spirit? The remembrancer. "He will bring to your remembrance all that I have said unto you."

He comes to us individually, and when He comes He isn't coming from without, He is coming from within, for He is buried within and He rises within.

"He chose us in Him before the foundation of the world." One man fell and became fragmented into un-numbered beings, all sons. Then comes the great affliction, the great tribulation of human experience. Then He calls us back one by one, but when we return we are the one who fell, who is God the Father. You are raised from the level of the fragmented being called the son, into the level of God the Father, who is personified, in scripture as Jesus.

About thirty-five years ago an artist friend of mine took me to the New York Library on 42nd and 5th. He was a member, and was able to take out forty-six pictures of Jesus. Do you know there were not two alike? They were simply personifications of the artists who painted them.

Here was the American Jesus wearing an open shirt, a radiant, blond youth. The Germanic Jesus would have enjoyed a lovely stein of beer. Here came the Italian with a sad face, and the French, he could have winked his eye at any passing girl. All these were the Jesus personified by the artist who painted them. Forty six, and each claiming to be the Jesus as he appeared to them.

There are those who will put these pictures on the wall and think it is a picture of Jesus. That's not Jesus. You will never *know* Him unless he reveals Himself through his son, and His son is David. When David comes into your world, you instantly know who you are.

Listen to the words: "I made it known; then suddenly I acted and it came to pass." It's a sudden act within you. It comes without preparation, without any warning what-

soever. When He appears you know you are the Lord
Jesus, with no loss of identity.

If your name is John, it is still John, but you know
you are God, the father of that son. And if David is God's
son, then you must be God because he is your son. You
know you are his father, and he knows you are. There is
no other way of discovering God in this world.

Someone came the other night for the first time and
told me about an esoteric society where, if you are a
member and you are born from above, the seed must
remain in you. I said, "You can sit on that seed from now
to the ends of time, and, if you are not literally born from
above, you are going to have night explosions, and you will
think you are doing God a favor? No."

You can have all the diets in the world, take all the
saltpeter in the world, do all these things and you aren't
going to stop the normal flow of that energy going down
into generation. When it is reversed into regeneration you
do nothing about it. You lose all interest in that impulse,
for the impulse is gone.

In the world of generation it is part of living, but in the
world of regeneration you are above the organization of
sex. It means nothing to you. You love them all, equally,
but you have no urge whatsoever to indulge in that which
you wanted so badly when you were turned down into
generation.

All the wonderful things we read in scripture are the
word of God, but they are only shadows. These are the
shadows of the reality. When the reality takes place it is so
unlike what the shadow appears to be.

You read the story of the serpent being lifted up on
the trunk of a tree, or the staff, and you think someone
called Moses took a serpent and lifted it up on a staff, and
all who looked upon it were cured. No, that was the
shadow.

We are told, "On this day, when he rose," (then crucified him and then he rose), "the curtain of the temple was
torn from top to bottom."

You may think of some temple, some cathedral or synagogue. But now listen to these words: "*You* are the temple of the living God, and the spirit of God dwells in you." If you are the temple, then the curtain must be in you.

The curtain of the temple is going to be split in two from top to bottom when that event becomes alive within you. I am telling you from my own experience, it comes suddenly and without warning. Your body is split in two from top to bottom. At the base of your spine you see a golden, liquid, pulsing living light. As you contemplate it, you know it is your very self and you fuse with it; then, like a fiery serpent you rise. The fire that went down into generation is now reversed into regeneration.

Who did it? You will say, "I experience it." So it's all in the first person singular. Listen to the statement again from the 48th of Isaiah: "The former things I declared of old; they went forth from *my* mouth. I made them known . . ." It's all in the first person I, I, I. ". . . then I acted and it came to pass."

Who is acting? Who actually had the feeling? I did. Who ascended? I ascended. Who fused with the light? I did. Who was split in two? I was. It's all in the first person. That's how God gives Himself to man, for God is the "I" of man. When you say "I am," that's God and there is no other God. But He sleeps in man and man is totally unaware of the true God.

When you hear the word God, the word Jesus, the word Jehovah or Lord, and in some strange way the mind jumps out to something other than the "I" of yourself, you have a false God. If you ever hear the word Lord and think of something external to self, you don't have the right Lord. If it in any way conjures some feeling of someone who exists external to you, then get back to scripture and try to find out who he is, for He is buried in you. "You are the temple of God and the spirit of the Lord dwells in you." Do you not realize that Jesus Christ is in you, unless of course you fail to meet the test.

If he is in me, what am I doing looking on the outside? When I hear the word "Jesus," am I going to think of something on the outside to come today, tomorrow or maybe a thousand years from now? If so I have the wrong Jesus.

Then who is the Christ? Christ is the son of God. Who is he if Jesus is not? He is David. He is the Lord's anointed. Did David not call him (in the spirit) my lord, my God, my father?

When you hear any priest, any rabbi or any minister speaking of the Lord on the outside, bear in mind they do not know the Lord. If you knew Him you would only think in terms of the I AM within you, for that's where He is buried.

Now the ultimate end is God giving Himself to you, individually. When you awake, you are God and there is no other God. But we are told to imitate God as dear children until that gift is given. It comes at the end of human tribulation. "How long, how vast, how severe these furnaces 'ere I find the father were long to tell." But He will try me in the furnaces for His own sake because He cannot give His glory to another. When He gives it, it is going to come suddenly, without warning, because the Holy Spirit returns and the Holy Spirit is simply memory returning.

We are told everything in the beginning, but we came down into the world of complete forgetfulness. After complete and total amnesia, memory returns and we know exactly who we are. But we know it individually because each one of us is so unique. Although we are one, still you are individualized, and not in eternity will you be other than an individualized being, yet one. We have the same son and we are the same father, but you are individualized, and this individuality tends toward greater and greater individualization forever and forever. That's the story.

But if I must imitate Him as a dear child, let me know my end, now. I do not mean the end of which I just spoke, I mean a temporary end. "I want to be successful," a man will say. Or a girl will say, "I want to live graciously in my world." That's an end. Now go to the end and view the world from that end. Don't think *of* it, for if you think of it you are not in it.

Now act in it. How would it be if it were true. What would the feeling be like if it were true. This is simply taking the end and drenching it in feeling. I assume that feeling of the wish fulfilled and I drench myself with that feeling. Then I open my eyes and the world denies it. It doesn't really matter. Let me remain faithful to that end and it will come to pass. Strangely enough I may pass through certain trials, certain heartbreaks and delays I can't quite understand, but, when I reach the end, the whole thing is fulfilled and I will see it was all in order. My own disappointments in my world led up to what I am doing today.

My father gave me five hundred dollars to go to a small school in New York City and the teacher made me the goat. She called me up before an audience of about forty students and said, "Now listen to him speak. He will never earn a living using his voice."

She should not have done that, but she didn't know the kind of person she was talking about. Instead of going down into the grave and burying my head in shame, I was determined I would disprove her. It did something to me when she said that to the class and used me as the guinea pig to show them what not to do. She said I spoke with a guttural voice, and this very heavy accent, and I would never use my voice to earn a living.

Well, I do not know what the others are doing, I haven't heard of them. There is not a thing wrong in selling shirts in Macy's; you use your voice there too, but I went home so annoyed and determined she was wrong, I went to the end.

I went to the end and actually felt I was facing an audience, unembarrassed, and I could talk and talk forever without notes. The class came to an end and we left. She was convinced, and maybe they were too, but it doesn't matter what *they* do, it's what I do. Others may be convinced, it doesn't really matter. The whole vast world is yourself pushed out. Maybe I needed that jolt at that moment in time.

I went through the different tribulations, and finally found myself doing what I always wanted to do, to tell the story as it happened to me in vision.

The first night I started I think six people came. I paid three dollars for the hall and wore a tux for the occasion. I stood up and spoke for ten minutes, then dried up. They were very gracious, all friends, and out of sympathy each gave a dollar bill, so at least I made three dollars.

That was my beginning. Then it grew from three to ten to twenty, and one night when I had about fifty, a man in the building saw me growing and growing and thought he would put a stop to it. He was going to one of these New Thought conventions in Washington, D.C. and asked me to take his platform. He had a very large audience of about five hundred.

I accepted his generous offer (I learned afterwards his purpose was to get me out of the place. He thought I would make a monkey out of myself before such a vast audience who were trained differently). Unfortunately for him and fortunately for me, the next time I spoke my room couldn't take them all. I had to move several times in six months and then to an old church which sat eleven hundred.

He thought he was going to hurt me, but as scripture teaches, "You meant evil against me but God meant it for good." So I got his audience.

You go through these things, and at moments things seem to be against you, but they are all for you if you remain faithful to the end. Let us be imitators of God as dear children. Then we are told, "I was not forgetful of the divine image. I remained faithful to it." If you remain faithful to it, let anything happen and then say within yourself, "You meant evil against me but God meant it for good."

I remember when people tried to take from my father

the little equity he had in his business. We thought the world came to an end that day, for he had a large family and no way to feed them or support them. He had ten children, his wife, himself, his mother-in-law, and a few servants. No one would come to see him because they weren't quite sure but what the accusation might be true. Yet, on reflection, that was the turning point of the family's fortune. From being a minor partner, having a very small equity in the business, he turned around, without partners, and transcended the wildest dream of the family.

He kept his vision. He knew he hadn't done a thing that was wrong, and he kept his vision concerning what he wanted in life and what he wanted for the family.

If you have a vision, and by vision I mean a day dream, remain faithful to it. What would you like to be in this world? Do you know it? How would you like things to be in your world? Well, that's a vision. Now remain faithful to it. Tomorrow you may be given a severe blow, and you may interpret that as being a setback. Time will prove it was the turning point in your fortune. Everything will add up towards the fulfillment of your dream if you remain faithful to that vision. It's all in your own wonderful human imagination. That's God.

God actually became as I am, you are, that you may be as He is. He takes upon Himself all the weaknesses of man. You may say, "God doesn't suffer." If you are in pain I may say, "Are you in pain?" You answer, "Yes, I am." That's His name. He has no other name. That's who He is. You may say, "I am in pain. I am embarrassed. I am unwanted," that's God's name. He is doing all the suffering, because He goes through life with you *as* you until the day He reveals himself as you. It is God and God alone who is playing all the parts in the world. There is nothing but God.

If God did not become as I am, I couldn't breathe, for He is my breath. But He doesn't limit me to my wishes, to my outlook on life; He plays all the parts. He waits on me just as quickly and as indifferently when the will in me is evil as when it is good. Therefore He subjects Himself to all the things in my world.

God is like pure imagining in you, in me, in every being in the world. You imagine? That's God. He waits on us because we imagine this, that and the other. Now you know this, go to the end. Make it a noble end, a successful end in your world. Having seen it clearly in your mind's eye, drench yourself in that feeling.

Now, tomorrow you may be disappointed. It may come tomorrow, but when it comes it is going to come suddenly and unexpectedly. But remain faithful to the end, and although things happen in your world that seem to deny it, everything will add up towards that end.

I am telling you this from my own experience. There is nothing but God in the world. The most horrible part and the most noble part He is playing. No one is greater than you are for no one is greater than God. Let no one pull any rank on you. You have a background that goes back to God. It's not a physical background; you're not a horse. If I am breeding horses I want to know their background. But you are not a horse, you are not a breeding pig or sheep; you are the unfolding of God and there is nothing but God.

I have had people tell me they have met Jesus, and, after they paint a word picture of him I say, "Who is he?" They say, "The son of God." "Then you must be God, for do you know in the 11th chapter of the Book of Matthew it says, 'No one knows the son except the father?' You say you have seen the son; then you must be the father, for no one knows him but the father."

Now listen to these words. "No one has ever seen God, but the only son who is dearest to his heart, he has made him known." That's the 1st chapter, the 18th verse of John. If you have seen God, then you must be the son, for no one has ever seen God, except his only son who is dearest to his heart. You are either Christ, the son, or you are

Jesus, the Lord. One or the other, yet they are one. One reflects the other. The son not only radiates, but reflects the glory of God and bears the express image of his person. When you look into the face of His son, he is the eternal youth, and you, the ancient of days, yet you are one. He reflects your glory, and your glory is simply I AM.

I tell you, the greatest book in the world is the most misunderstood. He said, "I declared these things of old . . .", but they were shadows. All these were shadows of reality. When he, himself, comes into the world and fulfills his own declaration, then his shadow world rejects him. It's not what they were expecting. "He came unto his own and his own received him not." They could not accept it because they were looking for some man on the outside to be a savior. No one on the outside is going to save you. God and God alone will save you. Listen to the word in the 43rd and the 45th chapter of Isaiah. "I am the Lord your God, the Holy One of Israel, your Savior, and besides me there is no savior. I am He."

It's not a being on the outside talking to you, I am speaking from within you. Your own wonderful I Amness, that is the Lord God Jehovah. That is your Savior, and besides him there is no savior. He reveals himself to you and completely unfolds Himself within you. Then He brings the only one in the world who could reveal Him as you, and that is His son. If His son is your son, then you and He are one. That is the story.

The end gives meaning to all that goes before. If I only know the end. The end is this, it is God's purpose to give Himself to me as though there were no others in the world, just God and self; not two, just One. He broke down the barrior between us and we became one. He cleaved to me, His emanation, yet his wife till the sleep of death was passed. Then I awoke as God the Father and there is no other.

Have your wonderful dreams. You want to be happily married? You want to be financially successful? You want to be known in your chosen work? All these things are but dreams, and if you know the law you can dream them into this world.

But when the visions come, and they are going to come, they will suddenly appear without any warning whatsoever. I know in my own case, these events came one after the other, and I had no inkling when I slept that a great event would take place that night, casting me in the central role.

We are told, "I acted, and it came to pass." *I* acted and it came to pass. *I* didn't see a being on the outside calling himself God, *I* awoke within my skull and found it to be a sepulcher. It was *I* who awoke. It was *I* who came out. It was *I* who found the little child wrapped in swaddling clothes. It was *I* who saw the three witnesses bearing witness to the event that *I* had experienced. It was *I* who heard the wind. The wind was like a storm wind.

It was *I* who saw David, who revealed my fatherhood. It was *I* whose body was split in two from top to bottom, and it was *I* who looked upon that liquid, golden, living light; fuse with it and then like a fiery serpent rise into my own skull. It was *I* upon whom the dove descended, and smothered me with kisses. It was all *I* as told in the 48th chapter, the 3rd verse of Isaiah. The whole thing is center-ed in the first person singular. Not "we," but "I." It's unique. That's the being you really are.

All that has happened to me is going to happen to you, so you may know in the end you and I are one. We are the Father; therefore the Father is a compound unity, one made up of others. That's what the word Elohim really means.

The first time it appears in scripture is in the very first verse of Genesis: "In the beginning God created the heavens and the earth." The word translated God is Elohim (plural). "God said let us make man in our image, after our likeness." Again, it's Elohim.

The Elohim is a compound unity, one made up of others. We are the fragmented one and we are called back into that unity. But when we are called back we become the One, the Father. There is no way to reveal you as the One other than the Only Son calling you Father, and you know it—for the Holy Spirit comes, remembrance returns.

Say what you want about the Father; say what you want about the Son, all that is forgiven. But to sin against the Holy Spirit is not forgiven. When remembrance returns you can't possibly deny it; therefore there is no possibility of sinning against the Holy Spirit.

You have heard all kinds of arguments that this means deviation in sex. What a lot of nonsense. It hasn't a thing to do with that. When memory returns you awake from total amnesia and you can't deny the being that you are.

Who is the Holy Spirit? "I will send you the comforter, the Holy Spirit, who is the Spirit of Truth. He will bring to your remembrance all that you have heard from me." Everything you heard before the world was comes back and you see who you really are.

I am telling every person in the world who will listen, you *are* God the Father. The day will come suddenly and without warning in the most unique, unpredictable way, and you will know who you are. You will know you are God the Father. Then, when the little thing called death takes place, you have taken off this body of death for the last time. Then you and I, in the eternal world, will be one in the most intimate sense, yet separate because we are individualized. That's something you can only experience when you are in that state.

How can two bodies fuse and actually, literally, become one body? I have had that experience. You could take the most intimate embrace in this world, yet you remain two, but when you are embraced by Love you become one. "He who is united to the Lord becomes one spirit with Him." You become one body with Him. You become *one* with eternity, yet you are individualized.

"Lord show me my end." Tell me my end and the number of my days, and he was told, "It is not for you to know the day or the hour, only the Father knows." When

that moment in time comes, it will not be delayed, it is
going to come suddenly and unexpectedly. Then your entire world is changed. No matter what you believed prior to
that moment, everything has been rearranged within your
mind, and you go about your Father's business knowing
you are the Father.

What is your business? Trying to awaken everyone who
is sleeping, because the Father is buried in every child born
of woman.

If you know someone who is on trial for the most
horrible crime, he is still the Father. If you hear of some
glorious person, he is the Father, but not any more than
the one on trial for his life. It's all God and God is playing
all the parts. In the end, when he comes you and I will
understand why. As the poet said, "Be patient, our playwright will show in some fifth act what this wild drama
means."

So when you meet any person in this world, regardless
of the pigment of his skin, regardless of his background,
you are looking at a mask behind which God hides His
face. He is buried there and He is dreaming there.

If you know it and believe it you can tell him how to
realize his dreams in this world. How do you realize them?
First, have a dream, and by a dream I mean a day dream, a
glorious, wonderful day dream. Then ask yourself, "What
would it be like if it were true that I am now the man I am
dreaming I would like to be. What would it be like?" Then
catch the mood of the wish fulfilled and drench yourself
with that feeling. Then for all of your tomorrows try to
the best of your ability to walk faithful to that assumption, and I am telling you from my own experience, in a
way that no one knows, it will come and it will come
suddenly.

When it happens you may even believe, as so many
people will, that it would have happened anyway. It
happens so naturally that people are inclined to believe it
would have happened anyway; and then discount the
principle and completely forget it; and fall in love with the

things it brought into the world; and worship the things rather than the principle.

Take away all these things, but leave me the principle and I will rebuild them. But don't take the principle and leave me the things. If you must take something, take the things, but leave me with the consciousness of how I brought those things into the world; and I will reproduce them again.

TRUST
IMAGINATION

I could tell you from now until the end of time that your own Wonderful Human Imagination is God, and you could hear it but never apply it. Quite often we cannot bring ourselves to apply it because it is in conflict with our training, but it does not operate itself, we are the operant power.

We are told in the 118th Psalm, "The stone which the builders rejected has become the chief cornerstone. This is the Lord's doing; it is marvelous in our sight."

Many years ago, sitting in the silence, my eyes closed in contemplation but not really thinking of any one particular thing, a huge quartz appeared before my eyes. Then it shattered, fragmenting itself into many, many pieces. As I watched, it quickly reassembled itself, but this time it took on the human form seated in the lotus posture. As I looked, I realized I was looking at myself. Then it began to glow, and when it reached the intensity of the sun, it exploded and I awoke in my chair.

The stone I had rejected was myself. I could not believe I, myself, was the cause of the phenomena of my life. I thought "he" did it, "she" did it, "they" did it . . . the world did it, but certainly I am not responsible. These things happened because of others, but I looked at the stone which the builders rejected. "It's the Lord's doing and it is marvelous in our sight."

When we see this world as a world of appearance behind which the reality of imagining lies, we find the truth. All things exist in the human imagination, and by that I mean the individual's imagination. In your own bosom you bear your own heaven and your earth, and all that you behold, though it appears without, it is within, in your imagination, of which this world of mortality is the foundation stone. It is the tree. Christianity is its fulfillment. It is the fruit, but the tree is Judaism, and all that it contains will come out, eventually, in a plan, a wonderful plan that was there in the beginning of time. That, we call Christianity.

Blake said, "I know of no other Christianity and no other gospel than the liberty both of body and mind, to exercise the divine arts of imagination." Then he adds, "The apostles knew of no other gospel and the worship of God is using his gift." Then he states, "God became as we are, that we may be as he is."

What is the gift? Blake also mentions that. He said, "Man is imagination, and God is man and exists in us and we in him. The eternal body of man is the imagination and that is God Himself, the Divine Body, Jesus."

As you are seated here, it's all about you. Your own Wonderful Human Imagination is the God of the universe. That is the one spoken of as the Lord Jesus. Is it really true? You are called upon to test it and see.

A gentleman wrote me a letter I would like to share with you. He said, "I am a psychologist, and I have wasted years trying to talk people out of their problems when I would easily have imagined them whole and happy; but I must tell you this story.

A patient of mine claimed she was abnormal in many ways. She and her husband had adopted a baby girl who, although now four years old, still could not speak. Then one day the woman said to me, "I do not feel abnormal anymore, so now I say to myself, 'I am not abnormal.'" I tried to explain to her that that was not the right approach and told her what happened to me.

I found a house I wanted to buy, so I began to imagine living in the house, when doubts beset me with the result that my doubts materialized into a person who had more money than I, and he bought the house. So now I know from personal experience that every person in my world only reflects a mood in me.

Then I reconstructed the sentence saying, "You must now begin to say, 'I am perfectly normal.' " She said, "I do not feel perfectly normal." Then I answered, "I don't care whether you feel it or not, you must begin to persuade yourself you are by repeating within yourself, 'I am perfectly normal.' " And she promised she would.

The day she began the child went into a coma. They rushed her to the medical center where within twenty-four hours she awoke, bright and alert."

She only bore witness to the strange claim of her adopted mother. But when the mother changed the pattern of speech within herself, the child was found to be not only alert but perfectly healthy and returning to a normal state in this world.

The whole vast world is yourself pushed out. "All that you behold, though it appears without, it is within, in your own wonderful human imagination, of which this world of mortality is but a shadow."

I know the truth of which I speak, for I have found him of whom the prophets spoke, Jesus of Nazareth. The world is taught to believe he was a man who lived and was crucified two thousand years ago. I am telling you he is crucified on humanity, and that one is man's own wonderful human imagination. That's Jesus, and there is no other.

He is buried in man, the dreamer in man dreaming this dream of life, and he is capable of anything in this world. Listen to these words from Deuteronomy, the 32nd chapter, the 39th verse. This is the Lord speaking: "I kill, and I make alive; I wound, and I heal: and there is none that can deliver out of my hand."

There is only one creative power in the world. The one who kills is the one who makes alive. The one who wounds is the one who heals, and there is no power other than this one power which is your own wonderful human imagination. That is God. There is no other God. He is buried in you and the day will come He will awaken. If I could turn you from this world of seeming reality to a world of imagination where you believed in the reality of your own imaginal acts, you would be on the verge of rebirth. When you can sit quietly, all alone, asking help of no one, and really believe that your imaginal act is a creative fact which will externalize itself and become a reality in your world, you are on the verge.

You are told, "Unless you are born again, you cannot enter the kingdom of heaven." The kingdom of God is within you and God is in His kingdom. Although He is in His kingdom and the kingdom is in you, you can't enter it unless you turn from this world of materiality (believing it is the cause, the reality) to live in your own wonderful human imagination.

What would the feeling be like if it were true that you are what you want to be? That they are what they want to be? That they have what they want? Don't ask how it is going to happen, the depth of your own being has ways and means your conscious surface being knows not of, but it will happen.

I can tell from the uprising of moods within me I am going to meet certain people, and I do. Churchill once said, "The moods determine the fortunes of people rather than the fortunes determine the mood." Catch the mood of your wish fulfilled. How would you feel if it were true? In spite of all things round about you that deny it, walk as though it were true, and, in a way you do not know, it will externalize itself within your world and you will receive it.

In the 19th chapter of the Book of Matthew you read these words: "With God all things are possible." Then we read in the 9th chapter of the Book of Mark, "All things are possible to him who believes." God is equated with the believer in man. The believer in me is my own wonderful human imagination. The dreamer in man. I go to bed at

night and dream. The dreamer and the waking I are one
and the same being.

My brother Victor has made a fortune. He loves the
very smell of a ship. He goes into his grocery store and
loves the odor of everything about it. The odor of all the
things in his department store affects him. He so loves it he
is in the mood of success. Like my brother, fall in love
with something that really excites you and feel you are
already what you want to be. If you do this, I tell you
from my own experience, you will have it.

They came to Jesus, (the embodiment of imagination)
and said, "You haven't eaten." He answered, "I have food
you know not of." What are you eating? What are you
feeding your imagination morning, noon and night? You
read the morning paper and react, yet you don't know one
character there. Before you get to the end of the page,
based upon some biased reporter, you react. That's what
you fed the Lord, for the Lord is your own Wonderful
Human Imagination. That's God and there is no other
God. That is the Jesus of scripture. That's the Jehovah of
the Old Testament. He is housed in you and that is why
you are immortal. You could drop this garment right now,
chop off your head, burn the body and turn it into dust; it
would make no difference to your immortality. You cannot cease to be, because God became as you are that you
may be as He is.

When we were children we had ducks, chickens and all
kinds of things you have on a farm. We had a large family
consisting of ten children (nine boys and one girl), a
father, mother and grandmother all living in our home.

Mother would say, "Take two or three ducks and
separate them, because in two weeks we are going to have
a duck dinner." What she meant was for them to have a
change of diet. When I was a boy, fish was plentiful and
therefore very cheap. You could bring in all kinds of fish,
but since we had no refrigeration you either used it for
bait the next day or fed it to the ducks.

We fed the ducks fish and they were fat and healthy,

but you couldn't eat that bird until you isolated it and stuffed it with meal, corn or anything of that nature. At the end of ten days their whole system changed, and when you cooked it, it was like a milk-fed bird. But if you didn't do it, you couldn't eat it, because, although it was a duck, it tasted like fish.

Start a new diet, and, just like the duck, it may take a day, a week or it may take you two weeks; but, if you persist, you will outpicture that change of diet and your whole vast world will change.

We are the only beings to whom He gave inner speech, and it is a marvelous gift, but you can't stop it. You are doing it morning, noon and night. You go to bed talking to yourself. We are always carrying on these little mental conversations with ourselves. But what are we saying? Are we arguing, or are we boldly affirming and asserting, "I am . . . (Naming what I want to be).

Remember, everyone in your world is yourself pushed out. They only reflect what you have been and maybe still are doing. Blame no one, not even yourself, just change your diet. The diet is simply words, all within you.

Assume that you are now the man, the woman you want to be. Walk in that assumption, live in it just as though it is true. Then, who knows, that diet may not take more than twenty-four hours—I am quite sure it will not take more than a few weeks, and it will project itself in your world.

You are the Lord and the Lord feasts upon words. He is the Word. What have you said to yourself in the past twenty-four hours? "I AM in want; I AM sick; I AM unhappy?" Change it! Completely change it and say within yourself, "I AM wealthy; I AM healthy; I AM happy!" Reason may deny it, your senses may deny it; no matter, persist and sleep as though it were true and it will become true.

I can tell you from my own personal experience it works. But, as you are told in scripture, "I have ways and

means you know not of. My ways are past finding out."
All you do is simply go on a new diet.

Blake once said, "O what have I said, what have I
done, O all powerful human words?" If man could only
realize what he is doing when he is thinking. After all, who
cares, or who knows. Who knows? The only One that
cares, knows, and He is your own Wonderful Human
Imagination. That is God. That's the Jehovah of the Old
Testment and the Jesus of the New Testament, and there is
no other God. He is buried in you and He is dreaming in
you, and one day you will awaken to the being you really
are.

The day you move into the life of imagination, trusting
your imagination and living in it as though it were true,
you are not far from the threshold. But I can't tell you the
day or the hour, for no one knows but the Father, and the
Father is your own Wonderful Human Imagination.

I saw it so clearly. This is the stone that the builders
rejected. But what the builders rejected has become the
chief cornerstone. "It was the Lord's doing and it is marvelous in our sight."

I rejected the fact that I was the cause of the phenomena of my life and thought everyone outside of myself
caused it. Then I saw the vision. Here is a stone, a quartz,
fragmented, then come together in the shape of a man
seated in the lotus posture. As I looked at it I saw it was
myself. Then I realized I was the cause. He is the dreamer
in me. One day he is going to awake from this dream, and,
when he awakes, I am he and he and I are One.

IMMORTAL MAN

Man is all imagination, and God is man and exists in us and we in Him. The eternal body of man is the imagination and that is God Himself. There is a vast difference between states and the immortal you, for the Immortal You is God.

God is playing all the parts in the world. God alone acts and is in existing beings or men. There is only one Author and only one Actor in the world, and that is God; and that God of whom I speak is your own Wonderful Human Imagination. That is the operant power in the world.

When I speak of God, chances are you think of someone outside of yourself. But if I speak of your imagination I am certain you will think only of yourself. That is the God of whom I speak, who is playing all the parts, and the lowest part is multiple tongues.

We are not linguists, yet two hundred million of us all speak the same language and find it difficult to understand one another, because we move towards a prejudice, a fixed idea. When we say anything, first we have to get through that barrier even though we are speaking in the same English tongue.

Let me start with a quote from the 8th chapter of Nehemiah: "They read from the book, from the law of God with interpretation, and the people understood the reading." Paul claims in his first letter to the Corinthians, the 14th chapter, "I would rather speak five words in my mind that I may instruct others than ten thousand words in a tongue." Five words just to instruct others. That has been my hope since I started teaching back in 1938 . . . to make it so clear there is no misunderstanding.

Let me state it clearly now. The spiritual states of the soul are eternal. You do not change them. You pass through them like a traveler. You start at the very lowest, the tongues, the confusion of tongues called Babel in scripture. We do not understand each other, so we war over strange, strange confusions. The second one is the administrator, the organizer. We organize the confused states for personal gain. Then Paul goes up for eight and defines the last one as the apostle.

Now, the one who played the part in the very lowest is still the very same one who is going to play that part when he is called as an apostle and sent to tell the true story. Do not identify him with the state called the apostle. While he is in it, he is going to play that part. But he is not that, he is the immortal self in everyone.

The Judge and the One he is judging are both played by the same Being. That Being the world calls God, but they do not know He is the only actor in the world. God only acts and is in existing beings or men.

You and I, learning how to create, create states to deliver others forever. But what we make we can unmake, for we do not make permanent states. We create a state and take a friend out of what he was expressing and put him into the state we create for him.

Tell me what you want and name it clearly. It's up to me now to create the state and put you there. What would it be like if you were now what I wish you were? Then I try to persuade myself you are that being. To the degree I am self persuaded that you are, I have put you in that state and you will externalize the contents of it. But what I made, I can unmake.

I cannot unmake the eternal states. These eternal states

are all within the human imagination. They culminate in redemption and redemption is preceded by apostleship. That's when you are called. The word "apostle" means, "one who is sent." I find myself in a state where I am called.

The night I was called back in 1929, I had no idea I had arrived at that state. I was called into the presence of Infinite Love and it's Man. Answering His question correctly, that love was the greatest thing in the world, He embraced me, we fused and became one body, one spirit. For "he who is united with the Lord becomes one Spirit with Him."

At that moment it was not enough to be called and incorporated into the body of God, but to be sent on a mission. I did not know that mission until it unfolded itself within me. It took thirty years. Thirty years later it erupted within me and the entire story of Jesus unfolded itself, casting me in the central role of the story. Then I knew who the one called Jesus really is. He is the culminating point of God in Man.

When man actually completes the journey and comes to the fullness of it all, he discovers he is the one he has been seeking all through his journey. But he comes to that at the very end. So do not let him brag; do not let him boast he is an apostle. Apostle is a permanent state. He is infinitely greater than all the states. He created these and they are permanent within man, within the human imagination.

When you arrive at that state, it's the last of the journey, for then you awaken and know who you are. These experiences give you the certainty that you are God. Read the Word you read as a child in school and you read it as something entirely different. You know the Book is all about yourself. It's not about any being but God, and you have found God within yourself and *you are* God.

But that God of whom I speak is your own Wonderful Human Imagination.

Tonight I want to show you how easy this is. It's based

purely upon motion. The first creative act in scripture that is recorded is motion. "And the Spirit of the Lord moved . . ." He moved. Remember, the Spirit of the Lord *is in* man. "Do you not realize that you are the temple of the Living God and the Spirit of God dwells *in* you?" He dwells *in* me as my own wonderful human imagination.

Now I go back to see how He first created. He created by a motion. I move from one state into another. If it is a state desired, then I have a sense of relief. If, tonight, I was financially embarrassed and then came into a fortune, what would be the relief? Of all the pleasures that man could ever experience in this world, relief is the most keenly felt.

The child is late. You said to be home by ten o'clock. So, ten, eleven, twelve, and there is no child. You love her dearly and think you are in control. "Oh yes, I can control my imagination, my mind, it's easy." Then comes one o'clock and there is no child, instantly you conjure a hundred and one things that *could* happen. Then you hear the key and she comes through the door. What is your emotion? One of relief. Just one of relief! So of all the pleasures of the world, relief is the most keenly felt. It comes in the creative act. Relief. Call it by another name if you will, but it is relief, at that moment of explosion.

The same thing is true when I move into a state. What would the feeling be like if it were true? Then I work myself into that state as though it is true. If I am *in* that state, I can't suppress the sense of relief. What do I do after that? Nothing! Just remain in the state. It has its own appointed hour. It ripens and it is going to flower. Don't be concerned, you are in the state. Now let it unfold itself in its own wonderful natural way. It has ways and means that no one knows. It's ways are past finding out.

I move myself into a state. I don't remain in the state I want to leave behind, push a button and think something is going to happen. I move. I move from one state into another.

These states I am creating, but I do not consciously

move in the spiritual states. They are automatically determined by my journey in this world. No one can sit down and conjure the spiritual states. If he thinks he is going to, he is only kidding himself. These happen automatically as man, who is God, moves through these eternal spiritual states. There are eight completely marked out in the 12th chapter of 1st Corinthians, and you are not going to change them.

I have reached the state called the apostle. I was called and incorporated into the body of the Living God. He is a Living God, not a God of the dead, for nothing dies in God, but nothing. Everything is alive.

Today millions went to the cemetery; their friends or relatives aren't there. That's an organized big business. Completely organized on the fears of people. That's not where anyone goes. You drop now and you are instantly restored to life, in a world just like this. The unfinished work you are going to finish. No one is going to fail because God is the operant power and God is your Individual Human Imagination. He is moving towards self redemption and He goes through these states, infinite states.

But you and I, we are intelligent enough to create a state. Someone comes to you and says, "I don't know exactly what I want, but I don't like what I have." All right, let him tell you what he has.

You wouldn't like it either if you listen carefully. Then you say, "Let us reason together. What would you like?" He comes upon something he likes and you, his friend, create a state to deliver him from his former state. How do you do it? Bring your friend before your mind's eye and see him with a nice big smile on his face. Have him thank you for what you did for him. Not a thing has happened yet, but you go beyond the present moment and appropriate, now, subjectively, the objective hope. You hope he will stand before your objective with a smile on his face. You hope you are going to hear his words, "Thank you so much. It worked just like a charm. You know when I saw you the last time I was up against it? Today it is simply

rolling and rolling in my direction. Everything is perfect."
That's what you want to hear for a friend. If you are
hearing that, you have moved him out of his former state
into the state you have created for him. Do this and you
cannot fail.

Prayer is not petition; prayer is giving thanks. You
don't get down on your knees and petition anyone outside
of yourself. There is no intermediary between yourself and
Self. You need no priest, no so-called healer; you need
nothing on the outside; it's all within Self. What would the
feeling be like if it were true? Catch that feeling and then
work yourself into that state, feel it and keep on feeling it
until all of a sudden you are relieved. There is a release
within you and then it's done. You can't do it a second
time. It's done.

Every moment of time I am always viewing the world
from a place. That place could be from a financial position
in my world; it could be from a physical position in my
world, you name it. I am looking *from* a certain state and
seeing confirmation of it.

How will I know I have moved? It's a very simple test.
Unless there is a fixed frame of reference, no one will
know that something moved. If I started moving from here
to the end of the room and everything moved with me, I
would have no reference to prove I have moved. Motion
can be detected only by a change of position relative to a
fixed object. It must be fixed relative to me so I may know
I have moved.

All my friends know where I am, who I am and what I
am. If I desire a change, my friends as my fixed reference
should know it. I don't ask anything of them. I simply
assume I have changed. If I have, then I have the faces of
my friends as a fixed reference. Let me conjure them in
my mind's eye and let them look at me. Do they see me as
a changed person or are they still seeing the one who
would like to change. Are they congratulating me on my
change? If so, then I have changed, for I see it reflected in

their faces, I hear it in their voices. That's what I want. Now that proves I moved. No one saw me move physically. I am still seated in the same chair, but I moved.

The whole thing is based upon motion, a psychological motion. We are living in a world of imagination and this whole vast outpictured world was first imagined. There isn't a thing you see here that wasn't first imagined.

Yet, as close as He is, we cannot find him. Why? Why can't I find Him as something objective to myself? Because He is the Reality I call Imagination. I see the fruits of my imaginal acts, but I do not see the Actor as I see the outpouring of His activity, for He is the Reality I call Imagination.

The God in you is your own Wonderful Human Imagination. That's the one you are going to know when you completely awaken. That's what man is basically hungering for. The awakening of imagination which is the awakening of God within him. That is the only God of which the Bible speaks. There is no other God.

"I went down to the potter's house, and there he was working at his wheel. The vessel in his hand was spoiled. But he didn't discard it; he reworked it into another vessel as it seemed good to the potter to do." That's the 18th chapter of Jeremiah. The word "Jeremiah," means "Jehovah will rise." He will rise all right. He will rise in you *as* you because He is You. There is no one else to awaken but God, and God is your own Wonderful Human Imagination. Now the word "potter" in Hebrew means "imagination, to determine." So I go down to imagination's place where he is working at his wheel. What potter? My own imagination. What are you doing, Neville? I am just spending a few minutes here and there. Then, it's spoiled. You will admit what you are doing isn't what you want done. Now, don't discard it; rework it. Rework it into another vessel as it seems good to you to do. Don't judge from appearances. You think because he is up against it he will be satisfied with "X" number of dollars? No, don't limit it. Put no limit upon the power of belief.

Can you believe he doesn't have the pressure on him anymore?

Put him there. It doesn't cost you any more to put him in that state than to put him in a little modified state. You didn't pay anything for it. "Come eat and drink without price. Buy wine, buy milk without money." It didn't cost you a penny to do it, so why limit it?

When you meet people of great wealth in this world and you have judged them because they have money, just talk to them for a while. Money hasn't altered their other states. They are just as stupid as they were before. In fact, I have gone to parties where there were several millionaires, and a lady will say to me, "See that lady over there? She's not just rich, she's stinkin' rich." In her language that meant multiple millions.

There is a ladies' club in New York City where they are all millionaires. If you could only see them walk out of that club after their big heavy lunches. If you didn't know these were members of that club with all the millions in the world, you would say to yourself, "Poor souls." You would think they were the women who cleaned up after the guests left. That's exactly what they look like. But they feel they don't have to put on any fancy clothes because they are above it all.

When my father ran his store and all the very rich women would come in, he would turn to one of us and say, "You know God is really merciful. Suppose she didn't have money." He never completed the thought; he always left it to us to use our imagination.

I tell you, prayer will be answered. All prayers are answered if you know how to pray. Remember, prayer is not begging. You don't petition; you give thanks. You aren't going to give thanks to something that isn't. But you must believe in God, as you are told, "He who comes to God must first believe that He exists and that He rewards those who seek Him." I know He exists. I hope everyone knows He exists. As Blake said, "Why stand we here trembling around calling on God for help and not ourselves in whom God dwells." Why turn on the outside to call upon God when He dwells *in* me. He dwells in me as my Imagination. Commune with your own imagination until you are satisfied it is done. Then go about your business and let it take its own course. Time will prove it and it will come out perfectly.

You don't beg anyone. You don't petition anyone. It hasn't a thing to do with so-called holiness. That is such an abused word. He is a holy man. May I tell you if anyone introduces you to anyone as a very holy man, turn and run, for he will fleece you. They come over here from India. You see them on the TV. The next thing you know they are getting five hundred dollars for a "special" course, and people that have more money than brains pay. Then off to India he goes with his multiple fortunes which he has simply taken from those who aren't given to thinking. You know, money doesn't care who owns it. They have it and will give it out to anyone who is called a holy man.

I have had experience with these so-called holy men. One little fella on TV was asked by a reporter, "Why do you advertise so much? You are always advertising, building up your own little personality. Jesus never did." Then in a little, high pitched voice of his, he started laughing and said, "That's why it took him so long."

May I tell you you have everything it takes to be the man, to be the woman you want to be? Don't pass the buck. Right now know what you want to be. Be definite. When you know exactly what you want to be, don't ask anyone if it is possible. Simply feel you are it. What would the feeling be like if it were true? Would my wife, my husband, my friends know it? Don't tell them verbally, let them know it all in your imagination. Let them see you as they would have to see you if it were true. Then go to sleep in that assumption.

I know from my own experience that an assumption, though denied by my senses and therefore called false by the world, if persisted in will harden into fact. That is a law. How else would you interpret this statement from the

11th chapter of the Book of Mark, the 24th verse, "Whatever you ask in prayer, believe you have received it and you will."

No limit has been placed upon the power of belief. It doesn't even say it has to be good for you. It leaves you entirely free to make your choice and take the risk. Because when you reap that state, you are also going to reap the consequences of it. Take your choice but also be willing to take the consequences of the state.

Go through life knowing they are only states. See a person in the gutter today, he need not be there forever. Take him out of the gutter in your mind's eye.

A friend of mine went to San Francisco to teach this law. Before he opened, he was walking his little dog. A man, crossing the street came over to him and said, "I am out of work, could you let me have a little money?" My friend said, "I'm sorry but I have no money." The man was very nice about it and went his way. But before my friend took one step he saw that man gainfully employed and felt the thrill of his employment.

A month later he was again walking his dog when this man approached him and said, "I don't suppose you remember me, but I want to thank you for not giving me money a month ago when I asked for it. Had you given it to me I would have been asking you for money today. But I got so mad with myself for being placed in the position to ask a total stranger for money, I went home determined to get a job. I am now on the job I got the day after I saw you and I like it very much; so thanks again for not giving me the money."

He did not know what my friend had done, but he had moved him out of the state of asking for money into a state of earning it. Having put him there, the man got a job the very next day.

You can try it. Don't pass the buck, but help everyone in this world. You create states to deliver individuals evermore. These are states you create, but the spiritual states of the soul are forever, and no one is going to change them.

When you are in the final state of the apostle, it doesn't mean you are better than you, yourself, when you are in that multitude of confusion. For God was playing that as He is playing the state of the apostle. But God is above all states and you are God. You are not an apostle forever. You play it at the final part of the journey and then you come out redeemed.

When you hit that state, you know you are an apostle because you are sent. It's only then you know you have been chosen for a definite reason. You are sent to tell what happened to you.

When I tell you David is the Christ, I speak from experience, and therefore I speak with authority. I tell you he is the only son, which is a resultant state of the journey you made through those eternal spiritual states. When you reach the state of the apostle, you are born.

When you read the Bible in the future, and I hope you will, always bear in mind that the characters depicted there are not individuals as you and I are. They are states of consciousness from Adam to the very end. When you meet these states of consciousness in vision, they are personified and you see a man, but it is not man as you are man. All these are contained within the human imagination.

When you encounter Abraham, you are going to see a man and you know he is Abraham. When you encounter David, you meet a youth, an eternal youth, but it's a resultant state. You are above all states, for you are God. Every being in this world is God and God is one. "Hear O Israel, the Lord our God, the Lord is one." You can never get away from that. That is fundamental. The minute you have two gods, two will become four, and four eight, and eight sixteen, and you have confusion in your world. There is only one God and that God is named forever and forever, "I AM," that's the being.

Everything unfolds within the imagination of man and that is God. From now on walk knowing you have the

right to become the man, the woman you want to be. You
don't need to hurt anyone to gain anything in this world.
Go out and play your part fully. Let no one pull any rank.
All ranks are only states of consciousness. The king and
the court jester are both played by the same being, and
that being is unseen by the two masks; for behind the
mask is God and God is simply I AM.

One plays the part of the court jester and one plays the
part of the king, and we honor the mask and bow before
the king, but that court jester may be nearer to apostleship.

We are told the Lord said to Samuel, "Go down to the
house of Jesse, for I have chosen one of his sons to be king
of Israel. When the first son came in he was a majestic
creature, and Samuel said to himself, "Surely he is the
Lord's choice." Then the Lord said, "I have rejected him."
The Lord sees not what man sees. Man sees the outward
appearance but the Lord sees the heart. Then he brought
the second, then the third, and finally the one who was
tending the flocks, which was David.

Now this is all a story. We must extract the meaning
from that story. He brings in a youth and no one thought
for one moment he would be the one. "Then a voice spoke
to the prophet Samuel, 'Rise and anoint him, this is he.'
Then, in the midst of his brothers, Samuel anointed him
with the holy oil, and the Spirit of the Lord came upon
him mightly from that day forward." It never left him,
therefore he never lost a battle. The victorious one called
David.

In the end he stands before you, for he fought all the
battles. You were the Lord of Lords within, but you didn't
know it, and he is the Father's only son. He stands before
you and he is your son. Then and only then do you know
you are God the Father. You gain all the assurance you
need when you see David, for he is God's son and he is
your son; therefore you must be God.

THE
MYSTERY
OF FORGIVENESS

The glory of Christianity is to conquer by forgiveness.
We are so apt to contribute our ills and troubles to outward causes, to our environment, the conditions that surround us, to things we desire and lack or undesirable things
that are present. While all the time the *real* cause is sin.

Now, sin is simply missing the mark. You have an
objective you haven't realized and after a while you are
frustrated . . . that is sin. The Gospel teaches that all ills
and troubles can be traced to sin.

Let us take the story as told us in the Book of Mark.
"After John was arrested, Jesus came into Galilee preaching the gospel of God and saying, the time is fulfilled, the
kingdom of God is at hand. Repent and believe in the
gospel." Now this drama takes place in the individual. It's
all on the inside after John is arrested.

We read the story of John the Baptist and learn he
wore camel's hair and a leather girdle and did violence to
his appetite living on locust and wild honey, believing that
he could acquire merit as millions today believe.

When man discovers that's not the way and arrests that
state of mind within himself, the new man comes. He who
is waiting to be awakened in man is born. Then he makes
the proclamation that the kingdom of heaven is at hand.

But he puts a condition now saying, "Repent and believe in the gospel."

He is the Gospel. He is the pattern man. He has experienced scripture, in detail, and knows he is the central figure. Jesus now interprets the Old Testament with himself as the very center of it.

For he said, "In the volume of the book it is written about me." He calls himself the Son of Man. You never find this title on the lips of anyone outside of Jesus, yet you'll find it scores of times in the Gospels.

Then they bring him a paralytic. Now a paralytic need not be a physical being that is incapacitated. You could have a paralysis of business where the merchandise is not flowing. If it does not flow and become alive, there will be bankruptcy. You could have a paralysis in your social world where you are not invited as you were. You may have a paralysis in the art world where you lose inspiration, the painting isn't coming, the poetry or writing isn't coming.

The paralytic represents paralysis in our world. All the miracles are parables, and a parable is a story told as if it were true, leaving the one who hears it to discover the fictitious character and then learn its meaning and apply it.

When he saw the paralytic he said, "Your sins are forgiven." The scribes and Pharisees said, "Why does he speak thus? This is blasphemy, who can forgive sins but God alone." Discerning their hearts he said to them. "Which is easier to say, 'Your sins are forgiven' or 'Rise, take up your pallet and walk.' But that you may know that the Son of Man has authority on earth to forgive sins I now say, 'Rise, take up thy pallet and go home.' " The man rose and went out glorifying God.

How do I put that into practice? What am I called upon to do? He started off by saying to repent and believe in the Gospel. Repentance and faith are the conditions of forgiveness. I can't forgive without repentance. Repent means a radical change of attitude, a change of mind, a reversal or revision of my thinking. I need not go down to the root, I can change a portion of it, but I must change my attitude.

If I can change my attitude towards anyone in this world, I can forgive them. Someone stands before me unemployed. I represent that man to myself as one who is gainfully employed. I persuade myself he is and to the degree I am self-persuaded, he becomes employed. I do not need the man's consent, permission or knowledge. I do not see the need. I simply act as the Son of Man is called upon to do. If I do it and get the results I desire, I have found who the Son of Man is.

The Son of Man is Christ and Christ is God. I didn't pray to any outside God. I didn't go to any individual and ask him for help, I simply tried it. I did what I believed should work and it worked. Well, if it works, then I know who the Son of Man is. We are told, "Do you not realize that Jesus Christ is IN you? Test yourselves and see." Paul is calling upon man to test himself, for in him is the Son of Man, the title most often used by Jesus of himself.

He confessed He was the Christ, the Son of the Blessed, the Son of God. He also confessed He was God. "He who sees me sees the Father, how then can you say show me the Father?" But the title most often on His lips and only on His lips is that of the Son of Man.

The Son of Man has authority to forgive sins. If you can forgive sins (sin is simply a man missing the mark) and don't ask the man's permission or receive his consent, he doesn't know what you are doing. You are moved by some emotion and instead of sympathizing with him and keeping him in that state, you empathize. You do it all in your imagination, for Christ is your own Wonderful Human Imagination. There never was another Christ and never will be another.

The cry on the cross, "Father forgive them, for they know not what they do." The cry of one asking forgiveness for what they are doing to him. You are doing it to

your own wonderful human imagination every time you
misuse it.

I misuse my imagination by indulging in some unlovely
thinking concerning myself or another, so I am saying forgive me, I don't know what I am doing or I would not do
it. I am pointing out to myself to forgive every man for
his misuse of the being that I am, for I am in you and you
are in me. We are one and our Imagination is this one
universal Christ.

"Father, forgive them" is the cry on the cross. There is
no other cross he bears other than the body you wear. He
became man that man may become God. I have proved
that He is my Imagination. What do I do but represent the
individual to myself as I would like to see him in the
world. I persuade myself that this representation is true
and in time it becomes real. When I see the law work, I
know who I am . . . I am He.

Everyone who is missing the mark is paralyzed and
frustrated but invariably blames outside causes. He points
to his environment, to conditions round about him, but
always to things. That's not the cause of man's ills or his
troubles. The real cause is man's sin. He is missing the
mark, and after a while he is frustrated, and frustration is
sin because frustration is simply missing the mark.

The glory of Christianity is to conquer by forgiveness.
If I do it morning, noon and night, I am putting into
practice what the whole story of Christianity is all about.
While I am here on this earth I have an authority to forgive
sin, waiting for that moment in time when I will fulfill in
myself the sacred history of Israel and bring it to climax.
When I do, I will know that the Bible was all about me.
But who is this me? Neville? No! It is my own wonderful
human imagination. It was all written about Christ and
Christ is my Imagination. Christ is the Son of Man which is
my own Wonderful Human Imagination.

This is forgiveness. Scripture is all about forgiveness.
"Peter said to him, 'Lord, how often must I forgive my
brother, as many as seven times?' He answered, 'I did not

say seven times but seventy times seven.' " In other words, until it happens. It is an endless number. Do it until you become self-persuaded the thing is done. For, until you are self-persuaded, you haven't succeeded in forgiving.

To forgive is also to forget. Man cannot forgive and not forget. Blake said, "In heaven, the only art of living is forgetting and forgiving." There is no other art. In hell, everything is self-justification. There is no forgiving and no forgetting. When the priesthoods of the world forgive you, meet you on the street an hour later and still remember your confession, they haven't forgiven at all. They have not represented you to themselves as the woman, as the man you would like to be. They see you as the one who confessed. That's not forgiving because it's not forgetting, and where there is no forgetting, there is no forgiving.

It doesn't really matter how often you sin and become frustrated. Practice the art of forgiveness and go through life forgiving. Forgive every being in this world, for they are not really to be condemned; they are in states of consciousness. The state is the thing, not the man. You lift him out of the state by representing him to yourself as being in another state. If you do it, there is no condemnation. A man has to be in the state of violence to commit violence. If the state expressed is undesirable, it's the state, not the one who is in it. He who is in it is the agent expressing the state. If you know this and bear this in mind, you will not condemn anyone.

All the miracles are parables and parables simply convey a certain story. The story of Jesus Christ himself is an acted parable. The whole story, from beginning to end, is dramatizing God's plan of redemption. One day you are going to experience that parable and then you will know the reality of it. The whole thing will erupt within you like a flower erupting upon a vine, and you will know the truth of the Gospels.

Jesus took the entire Old Testament and interpreted it placing himself as the central figure. That shocked every rabbi in the world, for that was not what they were looking for. They were expecting something entirely different from a normal man, moving around the streets of the world, uneducated and not anyone to hail, yet it happened in him and he told the story.

Those who followed him were also the uneducated. We are told in the Book of Acts that John and Peter began to do fantastic things in the name of Jesus, and the Sadducees stopped them. With their great political power they threatened them and told them never again to teach in the name or mention anything concerning Jesus. Then they said to those who would stop them, "Whether it is right in the eyes of God to listen to you relative to God you must judge, but we cannot speak of anything other than what we have heard." We have heard it and we have experienced it. What else can we talk about?

If the whole vast world rose tonight and told me that what I am saying is misleading and I must no longer talk about it, I couldn't. How can I ignore what has happened? I can no more deny what has happened to me than I can the simplest evidence of my senses. I know what I had for dinner tonight, but that is not as graphic in my mind's eye as the unfolding of scripture within me.

What happened back in '29 and then in '59 when the dramatic scenes unfolded are more indelibly impressed upon my mind than yesterday's meal.

Peter and John said, "If it is right in the eyes of God, you be the judge, we cannot do other than speak of what we have heard and seen." They went through life forgiving and forgiving, which is simply putting into practice repentance and faith. For repentance and faith are the conditions of forgiveness. I repent by changing my attitude, reforming the being before me. To the degree that I am self-persuaded, he will conform. The world hasn't seen it as yet, but I have seen it. Having seen it, I am loyal and will not violate my pledge. I have pledged myself to remain loyal to the state relative to you (or myself) and to that degree you will conform if I am loyal to it.

But repentance comes first because it means changing

or reforming what I see with my senses. I change it in my mind's eye. If it works I have found Christ. There is no other Christ, because by Him all things are made and without Him was not anything made that was made.

If you imagine and without any effort on your part or appealing to anyone in the world, it happens, you can reflect and say, "It happened because this, that or the other," and give all credit to the means, because the cause remains hidden. The cause was your imagination. Who sees your imagination? He is the unseen being in the midst of you whom you do not know. Whose very buckles you are not worthy to untie. Here is the one who will, one day, actually baptize you with the Holy Spirit. He will be so satisfied with what He has accomplished in you that He will actually come down in fullness and possess you and wear you as a garment. Then you and He are one. But in the earliest gospel, which is Mark, we are invited to start practicing repentance. This comes after the outer man has been arrested; when I no longer think I can get into the kingdom of heaven by doing violence to my appetite, not smoking or not eating meat, etc.

Sin is the cause of every ill in the world, of every distress. All the problems of the world are nothing more than sin. You will find it all through the Bible, "Your sins are forgiven, your sins are forgiven, your sins are forgiven." One came paralyzed, one came claiming adultery, one was dead and no matter what it was He said, "Your sins are forgiven." He represented them to Himself as they would like to be seen by themselves and persuaded Himself that this representation was true, and they became exactly as He, in His mind's eye, believed them to be.

Now everything said of the Son of Man, who is Jesus, must be experienced by you. When it is experienced by you, you are God the Father. He said, "He who sees me sees the Father." Oh yes, in the world of men I am the son of God, I am the creative power of God, the wisdom of God; but "I came out from the Father and I came into the world. Again I am leaving the world and I am going to the

Father." I return to myself, having come into the world
with all the limitations and return to the being that I really
am.

Let no one tell you God is not a person. I tell you God
is a person. You stand in the presence of the Risen Lord
and it is man. "Thou art a man, God is no more, thine own
humanity learn to adore." Infinite love, yes, but man.
Don't think of God as some impersonal force, think of
God as man. He actually is man. That's why you are man.
He became you. Now He is raising you to His glory, His
love, His power and His wisdom, all the things that He is.

Start now to practice forgiveness and start with a
simple change of attitude; that's repentance. Believe in the
reality of that change, that's faith. Remain loyal to that
unseen reality. That's your real trust, your real faith. Walk
in that state as though it were true and in a way you do
not know and could not devise, it becomes true. Henry
Thoreau said, "If one would advance confidently in the
direction of his dreams, endeavoring to live his life which
he has imagined, he will meet with the success unexpectedly in common hours."

Let no one say "When?" It's not your concern as to
when . . . you have done it. I imagine it to be. I am still
imagining it to be. I will continue to imagine it to be until
what I have imagined is externalized in my world. I have
done it and if I have done it, then let it come to be in its
own fullness of time.

WHOM GOD HAS AFFLICTED

"Whom God has afflicted for secret ends, He comforts and heals and calls them friends." In the 119th Psalm He said, "This is my comfort in my affliction, that thy promise gives me life. Before I was afflicted, I went astray, but now I keep thy word. It is good for me that I was afflicted that I might learn thy statutes."

Then we are told in the Book of Job, the 36th chapter, "He delivers the afflicted by their affliction and opens their ear by adversity."

Who does he do it to? He does it to Himself. Let us turn to scripture. The Book of Genesis is the seed-plot of the Bible. It's all there, but it's an adumbration, a foreshadowing in a not altogether conclusive or immediately evident way. The Book begins in this manner, "In the beginning God," then it ends in this manner, ". . . in a coffin in Egypt." In the beginning God, in a coffin in Egypt. The story is all about God.

Everything in the world is God. I am looking at God masked as I look at you, for behind that mask is God and the whole thing is done by God to Himself. "Before I was afflicted I went astray;" it's my own word I pronounced before I came down into this world of death.

Here is a vision of a friend of mine that might aid to the understanding of this mystery. She said, "I was Infinite

Spirit; there was nothing but myself. I desired to go out into the world, although seemingly there was no other world. I knew I had to have form to be seen and communicate.

I made myself an elongated box of wood, entered it and there was absolute darkness: a complete restriction, as though I could not concentrate or bring myself to any greater point of restriction than at that moment.

The box could see; hear; move; it could do everything I willed it to do. Then came that moment in time when I desired to leave it. I had experienced what it is to see, to think and to hear in this world of death. Suddenly I was again Infinite Spirit, Infinite Light, for I was set free. I found myself looking down on what I thought to be my bed. A group of people were bending over, looking down at a body on the bed. One said, 'She is dead.'

I thought, "Dead? Why that's impossible. That cannot die for it has never lived. Only when I occupied it did it seem to live, but it cannot die. They think the box is dead when the box has never been alive. The shock was so great I awoke."

It's a marvelous vision. We *are* wearing this box. In Hebrew, the word translated box also means ark, a coffin. "In the beginning God, in a coffin in Egypt." The first and the last . . . the beginning and the end.

God became man for a purpose beyond the wildest dream of the box in which God is now residing. He reached the limit of contraction by becoming man, that he may expand beyond the wildest dream of himself prior to the contraction. It's constant expansion of the one being that is God, and you are the being.

We are the Elohim. We are the gods that came down and assumed the limitation of man, and it is an affliction. He afflicts himself. "Thou also suffers with me although I behold thee not." Then the voice answered, "Fear not, I am with you always, even to the end of time. Only believe that I have power to raise from death thy brother who sleeps in Albion" (in universal humanity).

Buried in every one of us is God. His name is I AM forever and forever. How will I know I will awake? He has arranged the entire return to himself. He prepared the way for himself to return and that way is described in scripture. It's told beautifully in the Old Testament, but again it's an adumbration, a rough sketch.

The New Testament explains it but man sees it in a strange light. He sees it as secular history and it's not secular history. The whole thing is divine history. The story of Jesus Christ did not take place here, it took place within man in an entirely different sphere.

The story of Job is the story of every man. If you are familiar with it, you will remember he did nothing that should have caused the horrors that descended upon him. But in the last chapter Job is made to say, "I have heard of thee with the hearing of the ear, but now my eye sees Thee." Then God multiplied his gifts on earth. His brothers and sisters and all who knew him before came to sympathize and eat bread with him in his house, "for all the evil God had brought upon him." These are the words of the 42nd chapter of Job.

The word "Job" means "where is my father?" Where is the cause of the phenomena of life? Where is the source of it all? That's the Father. That's the search of every person in the world. He may not know it, but he is looking for the source, the cause, the Father of the phenomena of life. That's Job.

In the Old Testament you are told that God is a father. He singles out one person and calls that one His son. If that one is His son and that one stands before you at the end of your journey, then memory returns (for it is His only son returning in memory). We are the gods forming THE God. If in the beginning there was a fatherhood, then fatherhood implies a sonship somewhere. If that son stands before you and memory returns, you know he is your son and he knows you are his father in the fulfillment of scripture; then and only then do you know who you are.

I could tell you from now until the end of time you
are God and you are not going to believe me. You would
say, "If I am God, why can't I do this, that and the
other?" You do not know the purpose behind the affliction, the contraction that you imposed upon yourself. You
did nothing wrong to bring about this contraction; it was
deliberate on your part. We agreed in concert to dream the
dream of life, to come down into the world of death, so
we did. Humanity (as we see it) is part of the eternal
structure of the universe. We actually came down into the
part of the structure called man, entered man, and man is
death. Then we turned death into sleep and we are dreaming the dream of life. "Infinite mercy turned death into
sleep and then arose the sexes to work and to weep."

We are multiplying this form that is man, but you are
not the form you are wearing. You are not this garment.
You are God. Everyone in the world is the immortal God,
but this experience is essential for an expansion. There is
no limit to expansion; there is a limit to contraction only.
We took the limit of contraction upon ourselves and
became man.

My friend's vision was perfect. She saw an elongated
box. The word "box" or "elongated box" as she saw it is
called "aron" in Hebrew. It is translated "temple" or
"tabernacle," but the word really means "grave."

Then I read in the 3rd chapter, the 16th verse of 1st
Corinthians, "Do you not realize you are the *temple* of the
living God and the Spirit of God dwells in you?" I could
say, "Do you not realize you are the *grave* of God and the
Spirit of God dwells in you?" Now, the Spirit of God and
the Name of God is one, I AM. One day He will awaken in
the grave. He will resurrect from that grave and come out
of the restriction He imposed upon Himself, for the temple
of God is man.

Can you put I AM aside from yourself? You can't
stand apart and observe I AM: therefore you cannot see
God. You cannot see God as you do objects in space, for
you are the Reality called God. You will know God when

His son stands before you, and then you will know the words, "I have found David; he has cried unto me, thou art my Father, my God and the Rock of my salvation."

Only as this is experienced by you do you really know who you are, for you see the relationship of Father to son. No longer will you worship a God outside of your self, for you will know there is no one outside of self to whom you can turn . . . .

Blake said, "Why stand we here trembling around calling on God for help and not ourselves in whom God dwells?" He dwells in us as our own wonderful human imagination. "Babel mocks saying there is no God or son of God; that thou, O human imagination, art all a delusion. But I know thee, O Lord, when thou ariseth upon my weary eyes, even in this dungeon, (in this strange mortal form,) thou suffers with me although I behold thee not."

How can I behold the reality I am as an object other than what I am? I can behold objects round about me, but I am the reality beholding objects. Then how do I know who I am? I will know only when my son appears before me and calls me father.

I suffered from amnesia when I came down into this world of death. You are suffering from amnesia and have forgotten your divine being. You are God. There is nothing in the universe but God. There is no room for anything but God.

Listen to these words, "No greater love has any man than this, that he lay down his life for a friend. Now I call you friend. I no longer call you slave, for a slave does not know what his master is doing, but I call you friend, for I have told you everything that I have known from my Father."

Now we go to the poet Blake and these words are put into the mouth of the one who just made that statement. He said, "Fear not, Unless I die thou canst not live. But if I die I shall arise again and thou with me. Wouldst thou love one who never died for thee or ever die for one who never died for thee? And if God dieth not for man and giveth not himself eternally for man, man could not exist. So, God dies."

He dies by giving up the being he is, emptying himself of all that is his and taking upon himself the form of a slave, the form of that box, that coffin, and enters it. His name is I AM. Then he calls the box by a name and says, "I AM Jim," "I AM Neville," "I AM _____."

We go beyond his *real* name which is "I AM" and put a little tag on it; then we become so identified with the little mask we are wearing we don't realize who we are. And in the interval of that pilgrimage we are suffering from total amnesia.

One day, in the fullness of time, He will awake. He plotted the whole thing before He started. He has prepared the way for His sons to return, for the Father is made up of the sons. Elohim is a plural word which means "gods," but put together it is "the Lord," Yad He Vav He. Put everyone in the world together and they form the one God, the one Lord.

He has prepared the way for all of His sons to return. This time, when they return, they are God the Father. It's a complete transformation of the sons into the Father.

Then a new adventure. What it will be I do not know. When the curtain comes down and this dream of life is over we are no longer sons of a father, we are God Himself.

You are not the mask you are wearing, you are God. "Whom God has afflicted for secret ends, he comforts and heals and calls them friends. Before I was afflicted I went astray, but now I keep thy word. This is my comfort in my affliction, that thy promise gives me life."

The fundamental promise made in scripture is the promise to Abraham, "I will give you a son." It doesn't state it is God's son, but it is implied. The name is Isaac, meaning "he laughs." When that infant is presented to you he breaks into a heavenly smile; he laughs. Then the next is the son, the youth David.

The child is part of the play, of the drama as recorded in scripture. The day will come when everything said of

Jesus Christ you will experience in the first person, present tense. Then you will know who Jesus Christ really is because everything said of him will happen to you.

If you knew how old you really are you would say it's impossible. The bodies you wear may still be capable of siring or bearing a child, but you are not the body you wear; you are eternal. But you cannot measure your age, for you have no beginning, and you will know no end.

Anyone not geared to this way of thinking would think me entirely mad, for I tell you that you, born in this twentieth century, are the father of God's only begotten son, and that son is not flesh and blood. If you read the story carefully, he came in spirit when he called him my lord. Jesus said, "How can I be His son when He, in the *Spirit,* called me, My Lord."

This is not something that takes place in the flesh. While you walk the earth in a garment of flesh it takes place in you. But it takes place in a region completely remote from this world, for you are an infinite being. The day will come when the dream completely erupts within you and you will know what I have told you is true, for I am not speculating; I am telling you what I have experienced.

The story of scripture is a true story. The Hebraic– Christian faith is the fundamental faith. All the other little "isms" will lead you astray. The Old Testament is the seed plot; it is the tree and we who have experienced it are the fruit of that tree.

I could be the tree and not bear the fruit, but I can't bear the fruit and not acknowledge the tree from which I came. Studying scripture I find the whole thing in the Old Testament. The New is simply the pattern.

Not every verse is equal in value, not every chapter, not every book, but there is a pattern all through those thirty-nine books, and the pattern unfolds itself as told us in the Gospels. If you want to find the words, the Book of Hebrews quotes the Old Testament in every chapter. Follow it closely. Everything quoted is related to the pattern man.

But when you see someone afflicted, don't think he has done this, that or the other. Look into the world and you will see so many fabulously wealthy people, yet you know how many of them got their money; but not a thing is wrong with them physically, so don't judge the one who doesn't have it. When you see one who is afflicted bear in mind the words I quoted tonight.

"This is my comfort in my affliction. That thy promise gives me life. Before I was afflicted. I went astray. Now I seek thy word. It is good for me that I was afflicted that I may learn thy statutes." Then he delivers the afflicted *by* their afflictions, not *from*, and opens their ear with adversity.

When we read, "Ears thou hast dug for me," in the 40th Psalm, and, "In the book it is all about me," we know the ears were dug by adversity, for the one speaking is David.

When you read the 22nd Psalm, called the Great Christological Psalm, you see the adversity in it, but in the end the words are, "See what God has wrought." This is David speaking. He looks upon what he has done and promised himself he would do, and all the adversities phase into nothing. I'm not saying it is not a difficult time, but bear it.

In the beginning, before the foundation of the world we were chosen to play this part and be afflicted. No matter how long it seems to be now, when we awake it will be as though we had slept but a short, short time dreaming this dream of life. Then we awaken to eternity and leave the world of death, for it's part of the eternal structure of the universe.

My friend's vision was perfect. She created a box. Upon entering it there was unspeakable darkness and contraction. It moved; it talked; it saw; it heard; it did everything man thinks he does here in this world. Then freedom, and looking down upon what seemed to be her bed she heard a voice say, "She is dead"; but to herself she said, "That's impossible, it cannot die; it has never lived. It only seemed to be alive because I was in it."

You are making this body alive. Let it turn to dust, which it will one day, but in the end you are the immortal one. If what I am talking about now does not happen before that moment in time, you will be instantly restored in a body about twenty years old, in a world just like this, with perfect eyes, perfect teeth, perfect body to continue the journey until what I have told you takes place; for, as we are told in the 17th chapter of Luke, God is within you.

People are looking for Him somewhere in space saying there is some central son beyond any sons known to man. They are still looking for some outside being in spite of the words "God is spirit; God is light; God is love."

I can't begin to tell you how wonderful the Bible is until you experience scripture, and it hasn't a thing to do with what our evangelists are talking about. They see some little tiny Jesus walking around, coming out of space to shake their hand and all that nonsense. Jesus Christ is within you, and when He comes He comes from within you AS you.

We speak of Him as Jesus Christ and that is not a true picture. In the 11th chapter of Revelations, we read, "The kingdom of this world has become the kingdom of our Lord and of His Christ." Not Jesus Christ. Jesus is the Lord. Jesus and Jehovah have the same root, Ya He Vau begins both words, which is your own wonderful I AM. His Christ is the anointed. Who did the Lord anoint? He anointed David, the Christ.

If you are afflicted or those you know are afflicted, don't blame, don't judge; make every effort to cure them. Make every effort to relieve them. "Whom God afflicts for secret ends, He comforts, He heals and calls them friends."

The doctor, the dentist or any aspect of the medical profession is helping to relieve pain and make the body you wear more comfortable. Exercise that talent and seek the comfort they offer, but don't condemn the one who is afflicted, for that one is God.

Listen to these words from the end of Luke, "O foolish men and hard of heart to understand; was it not necessary that Christ should suffer these things and then enter into His glory? Then beginning with Moses and the law, He interpreted to them in all the scripture to their understanding, and when their hearts and minds were opened He vanished from their sight."

All this took place in a heavenly sphere, not here on earth. We are re-enacting the drama while we walk in these garments of flesh. Man's darkest hour was that hour when God the Father addressed us and told us His plan. Then God died, He entered these bodies and became invisible to us because He took up residence in us.

We cannot see Him as a Father external to ourselves because He is not even near, for nearness implies separation. If I say He is near me, He is not my very being. But He is not near, He became me; that's why I can't see Him unless I see Him in his son, for when I see His son I know I am He.

Man's darkest night was when God became invisible . . . that was Calvary. God became man at Calvary, that at Bethlehem man may become God.

AS
A MAN
SOWS

The law is the eternal principle, for "All things must bring forth after their kind." This is stated in the very first chapter of the Book of Genesis. It's the law of the identical harvest. "As long as the earth endures, there will be seedtime and harvest." He then uses the analogy of trees, plants, all things in the world you and I can see.

But the New Testament teaches us that we plant not only the seed of the tree, we also plant ideas. "Be not deceived, God is not mocked; as a man sows, so shall he reap." You and I are in this world of educative darkness learning to create, for we are God. God became as we are that we may be as He is. We are learning to exercise our talent wisely, but we make mistakes and the mistakes will appear in our world to show us what we have done, whether we have used it wisely or unwisely.

In your own wonderful human imagination all things exist. "All that you behold, though it appears without, it is within, in your own wonderful human imagination of which this world of mortality is but a shadow."

You are within me; I am within you. The whole vast world is within your own wonderful human imagination. Now what do you do with it? How do you construct it? It is an art, and like all arts we have to make every effort to discover how to use it wisely.

This great secret of imagining is the greatest of all

secrets man could ever put his finger upon. Let us take a
few simple approaches to it. Suppose I want a better job.
If I am in doubt, the world will tell me I am not qualified
or times are not right or things are difficult; for the world
cannot tell me anything other than what I am telling myself.

For a moment, let me ignore what my reflection conveys and ask myself, "What do I want? The world is telling
me what I have done in the past, but what do I want now?
When I know exactly what it is, let me dare to persist in
that assumption, the outer world will rearrange itself and
reflect that which I have fixed within me, and I will be, to
the eyes of the world, that man. The reality is in my
imagination and not in its actuality. This world seems so
real and we think this is reality, but it's not; reality is in
the imaginal act which we project upon the screen of
space.

There are numberless facets to this wonderful principle. I am now looking at you and you are all real, yet my
home is far more real to me than this room, for I only
come here twice a week for one hour, and I live in my
home almost twenty-four hours a day, seven days a week.
This auditorium is used by many people and my home is
only used by my family. Yet, at this moment, my home is
only a flat picture and this room a cubic reality.

Why is this room the cubic reality, yet I know so little
about it, and my home that I know so well is only a flat
surface? Because I am in this room now. In it I give it
reality, but, when I leave one hour from now, it becomes a
flat surface and my home takes on cubic reality.

Here is the secret. Man is all imagination, and God is
man and exists in us and we in Him. The eternal body of
man is the imagination and that is God Himself. Being all
imagination, I must be wherever I am in imagination. I am
not anchored to this little body I am wearing. I wear this
body as I do a suit of clothes. The day will come I will
wear out the suit of clothes and discard them. I will wear
out this little body and discard it too, but not my immor-

tal self who is my own wonderful human imagination, for I am not confined to the garment I wear that I may be seen in the world.

I can sit this little body down on a chair, and, if I dare to assume I am elsewhere and give *it* all the tones of reality, I am there. How would I know it? Think of the world *from* there.

If I assume I am in New York City, how do I know I am there? Let me think of the world. Do I see Los Angeles around me? Then I am not in New York City. If I am there I would have to see Los Angeles three thousand miles to the west of me, for motion can be detected only by a change of position relative to objects. If I feel I have moved, let me see it in my imagination relative to the former state.

I do the same thing concerning going up in the social, financial or intellectual world. Today my friends know me as a certain person. Suppose I desire to transcend that person, would they know me the day I transcended or shortly after? They would. I would be the same friend but they would see me differently.

I dare to assume I am now the man I want to be, whether it be a financial gain, social gain or any other kind of gain, and my friends know it. Let them see me, and congratulate me, all in my imagination. I rearrange the structure of my mind and then fix it. I fix it by sleeping in the assumption it is true. If this principle is true, it will appear in my world, for all things come forth after their kind and I am planting a new seed. That is the seed spoken of in scripture.

I must not deceive myself, because God, in me, which is my own imagination, is not mocked. If this principle is true that all things come forth after their kind, and I dare to assume I am the man reason and my senses deny, but persist in that assumption, I should produce the fruit of that seed.

I have done it unnumbered times, so I am speaking from experience. You can do it not only for yourself but for your friends. A friend may say, "Hear good news for me." Take his request and, to the best of your ability, lift it to the state of vision so you can hear him tell you things are as he desired them to be when he spoke to you.

This is the story of Job, when he turned from himself and prayed for his friends, his own captivity was lifted. How do you do it? You do it with your thought. It doesn't take long and it costs you nothing to bring a friend before your mind's eye, hear his voice, and feel the thrill that he has what he wanted. Then you drop it, for that was the creative act. At that moment you planted a seed. Where? In your own wonderful human imagination. You rearranged the structure of your mind and planted that seed.

Now, do you believe in God? If you do you believe in your own wonderful human imagination. You believe all things are possible to God? Then believe all things are possible to your own wonderful human imagination. That imaginal act will now externalize itself in the world and your friend will bear witness to the truth of what you have done. That is God's law.

Now the vision has its own appointed hour. It ripens and it will flower. If it seems long to the one who asks it of you, don't be concerned, don't let him disturb you; simply wait, for it is sure and it will not be late.

My old friend taught me that lesson vividly back in 1933. There was a deep depression in this land and I was a dancer. Who would pay a dancer when they couldn't eat? All of the theaters were closed, so what was I to do? I wanted to go to my home on the island of Barbados but I had no money, and I mean NO money.

I said to my friend Abdullah, "Ab, I would love to go to Barbados." He said to me, "You are in Barbados." I said, "I am in Barbados?" He said, "Yes, you are now in Barbados." I didn't understand what he was telling me at the time, but later I learned he was telling me that if I wanted something, I must assume I have it. I wanted to go to Barbados. So, that night I slept in Barbados. How? In my imagination.

How did I know I was there? I thought of New York
City, where I was physically sleeping, and saw it two thousand miles to the north of me. This I did night after night.
The months went by and I didn't see any evidence of going
home, so I said to him, "Ab, if I don't make the next boat
out (no commercial planes were flying on those days), I
can't go to Barbados." He said, "Who said you are *going* to
Barbados? You are *in* Barbados." Then he walked to his
room and slammed the door in my face, which was not an
invitation to follow him. That's how he taught me.

The next morning I awoke to find a letter from my
brother Victor under my door saying, "I have told the
steamship company to issue you a ticket and charge it to
me. The enclosed fifty dollars draft is to cover anything
you might need on the way."

I immediately contacted the steamship company who
informed me they only had steerage accommodations
available, but I could be transferred to first class after Saint
Thomas. I thanked them, went back to my friend Abdullah and said, "Ab, it worked." Then I told him what the
steamship company had said, and you know what he said
to me? "Who is talking of going to Barbados? You have
gone to Barbados and you went first class."

Well, what are you going to do with a man like that? I
went straight to the boat on the morning of the sixth of
December, and as I was ready to board the man said to me,
"Mr. Goddard, we have a nice surprise for you, we had a
cancellation, so you are now going first class."

Ab wasn't surprised. I wouldn't even call him to tell
him because he wasn't given that way. He was trying to
teach me a lesson.

"You believe in God, believe in me also." The one
speaking is God, the God in you. You can say, "I believe in
God," but do you believe in your own wonderful imagination? If the word God conveys the sense of an existent
something outside of you, you have the wrong God,
because you are the temple of the Living God and the
Spirit of God dwells in you.

If He is in me I must find out who He is and where He
is. I have found Him to be my own wonderful human
imagination. He will not fail you, but when it comes to the
law, you are the operant power. The promise is yours regardless of the life you live in this world. Whether you be
rich or poor, the judge or the one being judged, the murderer or the victim, no matter what part you play, the
promise is not conditioned. God promised to redeem himself when He became man, and God keeps His promise. It
is not conditioned by anything you do in this world.

The only condition is on the law. You must dare to
assume you are what you want to be, remain faithful to
that assumption and it will come to pass. If you are not
faithful, it will not appear in your world, and if you don't
assume it, it will never come to pass, for you are the operant power when it comes to the law.

Learn to understand and apply it. Why not live well?
Why not live graciously? Why not be a kind, generous
person? Why not be a gentlemen, a lady? These are tre-
mendous accomplishments for anyone in this world.

Try to find out what the law is all about because you
cannot deceive yourself. The law will not allow you to.
You may deny you planted what you are reaping, but it
couldn't happen by accident. "Be not deceived, God is not
mocked, as a man sows, so shall he reap," and you are
reaping everything morning, noon and night.

I may not remember my sowing and deny the harvest
that is mine, but it's there and I've got to accept it. I do
not know the characters spoken of in the morning paper,
yet I react and that reaction was, in itself, the planting of a
seed. I passed judgement on those I read about. Read the
gossip of the paper and you are passing judgment, and all
of your imaginal reactions are planting seeds that must
come to harvest.

I don't care what the world will tell you, you can be
what you want to be. If you dare to assume you are wanted
in this world, you will be wanted. I am an American citizen
by adoption and not a member of any club in this land,

yet I have gone as an honored guest to almost every one of them because I never barred myself. It never occurred to me that I didn't have all of the qualifications to enter as a guest. You can go any place in this world if you don't put barriers on yourself. It's entirely up to you. God in you is your own Wonderful Being called Imagination.

Exercise it morning, noon and night and you will bear the fruit of your imagining. Not everything takes a month or a year to grow, some things come up overnight. You can plant now, this very moment, by daring to believe you are what reason denies and your senses deny. Feel it, give it the tones of reality and then drop it. You won't have to pick it up tomorrow morning to see if it's growing; accept it, and in its own good time it will come to fruiting in your world. That is the law.

The promise is yours regardless of whether you are rich or poor. But in this world of Caesar I must have the money Caesar demands. I must meet my obligations to life: rent must be paid, clothes bought, food, transportation, all of these are paid for by Caesar's coin, so I use the law for that purpose.

I have no desire to be a millionaire, but I do desire the comforts that a nice steady flow of income allows, without the anxiety that must come to everyone when he can't meet his obligations to life. So I use the law for that purpose and for my friends. How do I do it?

I sit in a comfortable chair or recline on the bed and think of what I want either for myself or a friend. I see him as he would like to be seen, and, in a matter of seconds, I work myself up to a pitch that something goes out of me. It's an actual feeling like some energy going out. It's a creative act. Then I drop it. You don't repeat the creative act after you have reached the point of explosion. Now let that seed grow in its own wonderful manner and externalize itself in the world.

I call that the subjective appropriation of the objective hope. You tell me what you would like to be . . . that's your hope. Now, my appropriation, subjectively, of your objective hope is all I do.

You are told in the 14th chapter of John, "You believe in God, believe also in me, for I and my Father are one. He who sees me, sees the Father." He sent you into the world, and the sender and the sent are one, but in the world you seem to be inferior to yourself, the sender, so you too can say, "I and my Father are one, but my Father is greater than I."

You are not inferior to your essential being, who is Father, but in the office of the sent you are handicapped. Trust your own wonderful human imagination. Start now, from where you are, and go as far as you want to. You have no handicaps other than the handicaps you put upon yourself.

Don't accept limitation. Go about your business of applying this eternal principle that all things must bring forth after their kind. Remember, you have the choice of the seed you plant. Plant a good seed or a bad seed; it's entirely up to you.

If you want money, make it money. Don't fall in love with it, but assume it is coming in a normal, natural way, without knowing from whom or where. Just go to the end and live as though it were true, and may I tell you it will be true.

But, set your hope fully upon the grace that is coming to you as the revelation of Jesus Christ in you. Jesus Christ is the Lord and His Christ. Not one name as it were, but the Lord's Christ is David.

Let me close with a little poem Browning wrote concerning David. He was inspired by the 17th chapter of 1st Samuel. Standing before the insane King Saul is the youth David, and David said to him, "O Saul, a face like my face shall receive thee; a Man like unto me thou shalt love and be loved by forever; a Hand like this hand shall throw open the gates of new life to thee. See the Christ stand!"

Who is David addressing? Humanity who has forgotten who he is. That's a form of insanity called amnesia. We have forgotten we are God, so we are Saul, and in that state of consciousness we are called insane, demented. Then the Christ stands before us and He is David. "A face like my face," said He, "shall receive you. A Man like unto me thou shalt love and be loved by forever. A Hand like this hand shall throw open the gates of new life to thee. See the Christ stand!"

May I tell you, when you see the Ancient of Days you will be incorporated into His body. He will embrace you and you will become one body, one spirit with the Ancient of Days.

I am not an artist, but when you see David He is the image of the Ancient of Days, but he is Eternal Youth. David sees his Father. He is the image of his Father, only young, and you, incorporated into the Ancient of Days, are God the Father. That's why David recognizes you as his Father.

This the the final revelation of God to man. "In many and various ways God spoke of old to our fathers by the prophets, but in these last days He has spoken to us by His son." Then you will know the end has come. You are the Ancient of Days in an entirely different realm, yet dwelling within all.

KEEP
THE
SABBATH

"God saw everything He had made, and, behold, it was very good. And God rested on the seventh day from His work which He had made."

We are told the seventh day is a day for man to observe. It's part of the creative act of God. The unknown author of the verse I have just quoted connects the Sabbath with the creative act of God. Without it, there's no creation. "The seventh day is the Sabbath of the Lord your God and in it you shall not do any work." That is the creative act.

If one commandment is treated imaginatively, then all commandments must be treated in the same manner. The Old Testament is a prophecy of all that must take place in the individual and fulfilled in what we have as the New Testament. The New Testament interprets the Old, not the other way around. You can't understand the Old without the New. When the time was fulfilled, He unfolded in the individual and we have what is known as the New Testament.

In the New Testament, we have one of the ten commandments analyzed for us. "Thou shalt not commit adultery, but I say unto you, any man who has looked upon a woman lustfully has already committed the act of adultery with her in his heart." That is, to imagine the act, to desire it, is to have performed the act whether you do it physically or not. That is one commandment (I could take all ten) as given to us in the Sermon on the Mount.

We are called upon to keep the Sabbath . . . in it we shall do no work. What is the Sabbath? First of all, God creates and He is invisible. God calls a thing not seen as though it were. Then He keeps the Sabbath and the unseen becomes seen. That which is subjective becomes objective only by the keeping of the Sabbath. It's part of the creative act.

I imagine a scene just as I would like it to be. Perfect! Wouldn't it be wonderful if it were true? Now, can I keep the Sabbath? We all break it morning, noon, and night.

Friday evenings, the Orthodox Jew keeps the Sabbath, and on Sunday millions of Christians will "so-called" keep the Sabbath. They're not keeping the Sabbath. Listen to the words, "Formerly when you did not know God you were in bondage to beings who, by nature, are no gods; but now that you know God, or rather that you have come to be known by God, how can you turn back? You observe days and months and seasons and years; I'm afraid I have labored over you in vain."

We think we keep the Sabbath. I go to my barber, and the shoe shine boy, a very nice chap, is a deacon in his church. I will say to him, "How are things going?" He will say, "I spent the whole day, Sunday, in church. I went from one church to another and didn't get home till 6:30." He thought he kept the Sabbath.

My sister thinks she keeps the Sabbath by going to church on Sunday. When I was a boy, there were certain things you couldn't do on the Sabbath. When I was a dancer I loved playing Boston because I got paid for Sunday, although I couldn't work, as the law forbade dancing on Sunday. The same was true in Philadelphia. You can't play baseball in New York on Sunday until the afternoon, so the people can go to church in the morning. Bars can't be opened until after one because then you wouldn't go to church. Who is kidding who? Is that the sabbath?

It hasn't a thing to do with the Sabbath. The Bible is the most practical book in the world if you only understand what it is talking about. "The seventh day is the Sabbath of the Lord, your God." These are the words. Not just the *Lord* but the Lord, your God, and in it you must not do any work.

A friend of mine wrote me a letter. She said, "I sell homes. I had an empty home for sale and the need for the sale of this home is great. I've found it easy now to imagine, because I've proved time and time again that imagining creates reality, so it becomes easier and easier to go to the end of an imaginal act which implies the fulfillment of my desire, and then rest. Yet, in this case, I found myself going back, wondering who would be a buyer. I couldn't stop thinking of a buyer and realized I was not resting in the end. If I've gone to the end and it's sold, then why am I thinking of a buyer? To me that was a confession; I was not dwelling in the end and resting in that state."

Then she had three dreams in the same night, all of them related. In the first one she dreamed she drove up to the house. A voice said, "What are you doing here? The house has been sold because you desired it." In the dream she felt a little bit uneasy. The house had been sold and here she had driven up to the house, undoubtedly because of her concern. Now the dream changes, and she is boiling rice and eager to get the rice done, instantly. So, instead of slowly cooking it until it is prepared, she put it in a pot of water, turned the flame high and demanded that the rice be done right away. Before her eyes, it was done . . . instantly done. She tasted a kernel and it was hard and tasteless; it was a mess.

Then she is preparing lima beans and she has all the time in the world. She soaks them, and, when they are full and ripe and bursting, she puts them in a pot over a very low flame, knowing that if it takes all day, it's all right because there is no hurry; there's plenty of time. She looks again and the beans are cooked perfect; they couldn't be

more tasty, just beautiful. Then she saw the beans and the
rice together, the beans so tasty and the rice so tasteless.
Looking at them she said, "Isn't it strange? They both
seemed to take the same length of time." One she had
prepared so slowly and the other she had demanded to be
done instantly.

God, your own wonderful I Amness, the Father in
you, speaks to you through the medium of dreams. He
instructs you. He shows you what you are doing and
allows you to see it and learn how to correct it. You have a
house to sell. You have gone to the end, you have seen the
people occupy it and are happy; therefore, the sale is over.
But then she found herself during the course of the day
breaking the Sabbath. Fantastic promises are made in
scripture to those who keep the Sabbath, because it's part
of the creative act.

All things are possible to God. I mean the God in you;
I'm not speaking of a god in space, a god in time; I'm
speaking of the ONLY God, the God that became you that
you may become God. I'm speaking of that God which is
the only God. He is in you as your own wonderful human
imagination. But here is the creative act and these ten
commandments must be taken imaginatively.

You have committed adultery. Haven't you passed any
person in this world and not desired to know them and
strip them? Being a man undoubtedly I did, but I speak for
humanity; I speak for every man and woman in the world.
We have all broken the law of the commandments; we have
all broken the Sabbath. I haven't broken the other commandment at my age, but today I break the Sabbath.

If the thought occupies the mind and it's not really
pressing like the selling of a house, I may keep the Sabbath
beautifully like this. A man wrote saying that when his son
was about two years old, he and his wife discussed the
possibility of sending him to a prep school back East,
Philip Exeter. I know Philip Exeter but I never went there;
it is a marvelous prep school. He wondered, at the time,
how he could do it, thinking purely in terms of finances;

however, that was approximately eleven years ago. In the interval, he said he had not once thought of it. The boy has gone to public school here in Los Angeles; he is brilliant and everything he desired.

Yesterday he received a letter with an offer for the son to attend Andover, a scholarship. He discussed it eleven years ago and kept the Sabbath. It wasn't a pressing thing so they did nothing about it, and then suddenly it appeared in their world. What seemed to be such a sudden thing was only the emergence of a hidden continuity. It was implanted beautifully, without pressure. It took the interval of eleven years to ripen, until the boy reached the age where he was old enough to attend a prep school, and he received a scholarship to one of the finest prep schools in this country or in the world. He had kept the Sabbath unwittingly.

This lady who told me the story and had the dreams broke the Sabbath, but she caught it, and the depth of her own being spoke to her and told her how she was breaking it and how to correct it. She had two dishes, one she took time to cook, the other she wanted done right now. Let it be. Take time. It will be so perfect if you let it come to pass without forcing it, represented by the perfect lima beans. If you try to force it, there will be all kinds of difficulties and unpleasantness, represented by the tasteless, hard rice.

You do the creative act and judge it as perfect. No matter what it is in this world you want, it is created in you in the same way the God in you created the whole vast universe. I'm not speaking of two gods. When I speak of the God in you, I'm speaking of the same God that created and sustains the whole vast universe. There's only one God. "Hear O Israel, the Lord, our God the Lord is One," only one, not two. "He calls a thing that is not seen as though it were and the unseen becomes seen."

The God in man does the same thing. I want to be successful. I toy with the idea; what would it be like if it were true? Then I create a scene implying it is true. I accept the reality of that imaginal state and keep the Sabbath. *The creative act is not completed until the Sabbath is kept.*

A pair of doves have a nest outside my window. They go away occasionally, confident that the eggs in the nest are all right during the time they are gone. One day the shells will break and out will come little doves. So you and I, in confidence, simply imagine a state, regardless of what that state may be.

Now you may say, "Suppose I die tonight." May I tell you there is no death. You wonder why everyone has such different beginnings in the world? Because this is not the beginning at all. You didn't begin in your mother's womb and you don't end in the grave. If I make my exit as the world calls death, I don't die. You are told, "Neither death nor heights, but nothing can separate me from the love of God," but nothing in eternity can separate me from the love of God.

Now I am talking to myself, "Never would you have made anything had you not loved it." That's what we are told in the Book of Wisdom. Not one thing would you have made had you not loved it, and nothing can separate me from the love of God. Here I am, put in a world to create as my Father creates and finally I awaken as my Father Himself.

I may make my exit tonight with an unfulfilled desire, which I think I am eager to see realized. It doesn't matter, for I will realize it. I will find myself in a world just as solid and real as this, and all of my dreams will come to pass in the world into which I go. I will still realize all that I keep the Sabbath relative to.

The commandments are not to be understood as you formerly did when you did not know God. Listen to the words from the 4th chapter of Galatians, "Formerly when you did not know God," (there was a time when I did not know God) "you were in bondage to beings that, by nature, are no gods." Like the stars, like monkey bones, like anything outside of God. When I turn to it for com-

fort, I am turning from God. When I didn't know Him I
turned to everything in the world that offered me some
comfort, but now that I have come to know God, or
rather, to be known by God, I cannot turn back.

Now and then we turn back. How do we turn back?
We observe days, months and years. We know we observe
days; we know we observe months, for this is the season of
Lent when people give up all sorts of things . . . my
brother-in-law has given up pickles. Last year was the
ecumenical year which was observed all year. So we have
days, months, seasons and years, all kinds of things that we
worship.

That in itself tells you that no matter who they are
they do not know God. If he calls himself a pope or arch-
bishop or the little one who scrubs the floor, he observes a
day, a month, a season or a year. He does not know the
only God. It's told so clearly in scripture in the 4th chapter of Paul's letter to the Galatians.

Even if I do break the Sabbath, I can still go back to it.
She broke it, but God is a merciful God. If I were pure,
never would I have known there was such a thing as a
merciful God. I know I will be pure as my Father in heaven is pure, for I came out. You are told in the 19th
chapter of Leviticus, "You must be holy; for I, the Lord,
your God am holy." You can't escape it; for I, the Lord,
your God am holy.

You are told in the Sermon on the Mount, "You shall
be perfect as your Father in heaven is perfect." I have no
doubt that this perfection, this holiness, must come
because I, by this statement, have the potentiality. I possess the potentiality of becoming as God, becoming one
with him. It does not say you *must* be perfect as your
Father in heaven is perfect. He confesses he is not yet
when he makes the statement, but he also tells me I possess the potentialities of becoming perfect and, therefore,
as God.

I am told in Leviticus, "You must be holy; for I, the
Lord, your God am holy." Here is a promise. I know I did

it but I break the Sabbath. I come back, having broken it, and he is so merciful. He shows me exactly what I have been doing. He speaks to me. "What are you doing here, the house is sold!" Then He tells me why it is sold, "Because you desired it."

Desire is the springboard of success. I desire success. That's the springboard of action. I desire. What's his name? I AM, that's his name. I want to be successful. It is God in me asking me to create that state. So I create it and then judge it perfect.

You create a beautiful home. See it in your mind's eye. But you have no money to build it. Wouldn't it be wonderful if it were true? Now, keep the Sabbath and don't concern yourself with money. It doesn't matter what it takes or how it comes about, just keep the Sabbath relative to it. It will come to pass. You'll live in it. Then you'll tire of it and drop it just like a leaf.

A friend of mine told me this wonderful statement, "If you had but a dollar and it was necessary to spend it, do it as though it were a dry leaf and you the owner of unbounded forests." Live that way, just as though it were true. Spend it as though it were a dry leaf and you the owner of unbounded forests, and you will find that the money will come like the forest dropping its leaves. But, if you hold on to it, it's like your lack of confidence in the abundance of God and His ability to constantly produce.

God is a creator. He didn't make the world and then go sound asleep and rest. Every time I imagine, God is active. If I'm afraid, it's God's action, for God is my imaginal activity. *Every time I imagine it is God in action.* "He who watches over Israel," we are told, "neither slumbers nor sleeps." Yet there must be that moment of rest relative to that which I have judged perfect. "God created and behold it was good, and very good. Then God rested on the seventh day from all His work which He had done."

Nothing comes unto me unless I call it. Whether I need it now or in unnumbered years to come, I can only meet what I have kept the Sabbath relative to, for the Sabbath is

part of the creative act of God. When it happens, I may
not relate it to anything I've done, but it could not possibly come unless I kept the Sabbath relative to it.

My secretary, Jack Butler, died in 1946. He used to
have nightmares based upon W. Randolph Hearst's "Yellow Peril." He would read it, believe it and see the Japan-
ese swimming across the bay. Well, we have had a war with
Japan. Jack was so confident Mr. Hearst was telling the
truth. No, he was selling papers. He would put out scare
headlines, and people would buy the papers, read them
and believe them. It was all to sell advertising, that's the
entire press.

But keep the Sabbath relative to something. I'd suggest
you keep the Sabbath relative to God's promise. His
promise is that you will be born again because you must be
born again. In the 3rd chapter of John He says, "Unless
you be born again, you cannot enter the kingdom of heaven." It's the new age. You'll continue, you won't die even
though men call you dead, you will not die.

Keep the Sabbath relative to God's eternal promise
that you must be born again. How? God is keeping that
promise in the depths of your soul. Accept it, even though
you are in prison or horrible things happen to you judged
by human standards, still keep the Sabbath relative to the
promise. "You must be born again;" therefore, I will be
born again. Go blindly on in your assumption "I will be
born again."

There are millions in the world who think they are
born again because of a seemingly little change in their
outward pattern. In last Sunday's New York Times, there
was a story of a man, a Baptist, who was just arrested and
given seven years for breaking into the Baptist church. The
elders of the church said he was only baptized that day.
Just baptized, and after the baptism, he saw a great opportunity for self gain and broke into the church. And people
think baptism means something. It hasn't a thing to do
with reality.

There's only one baptism, the baptism of the Holy

Spirit. When you stand in the presence of the Risen Christ, He embraces you. You are incorporated into His body and you are one with the body of Christ. No one with mortal eyes sees you thereafter; they see the same garment they saw before. But you sleep in that body; you wake in that body; you walk in that body. Though you are ill, though you are this, that or the other, the body that you really are is the body of the Risen Christ. No mortal eye can see it, but you see it and feel it and know the being you are. That's baptism, baptism with the Holy Spirit. Then you go through the entire series of events of the Risen Christ . . . the birth, resurrection, discovery of the Fatherhood . . . everything concerning Jesus Christ.

Now, keep the Sabbath relative to it, and you will find it will come upon you just as suddenly as the offer of the scholarship came upon this father and mother for their son, who is now eligible to enter Andover. Nothing happens by chance in this world. There is a law behind everything. It all started somewhere and someone kept the Sabbath relative to that act. If I broke a fertilized egg before letting it rest for the normal interval of time, the chick couldn't break the shell and come out. Give me the most fantastic idea, clearly fertilized, and I will break it by not resting, and it becomes an addled egg.

Dream the most glorious, noble dreams and then rest relative to the state you judge perfect. Listen to the words, "God saw everything that He had made and, behold, it was very good, and God rested on the seventh day from all His work which He had done."

The word "Sabbath," which is the seventh day, is divine perfection in scripture. The Sabbath means "to cease, to desist from, to be at an end." I always start at the end. The end determines the means by which it will be fulfilled, but I must rest in the end and keep the Sabbath.

The first Psalm begins with a blessing, a benediction placed upon one who keeps the Sabbath. It's part of the creative act and you can do no more. You've done it and the feeling is one of complete relief. Of all the pleasures of the world, relief is the most keenly felt. You perform a creative act, you reach the point of climax, then there is relief. You can't continue in the act because it's done. Now, can you keep the Sabbath after you've reached the climax? You've seen it clearly in your mind's eye. You have constructed a scene which would imply the fulfillment of your dream and you bring yourself to the point of complete explosion; then you drop it; you have fertilized it and that's all that needs to be done. Go about your Father's business creating other things, not waiting anxiously like the rice dish, but going about like the lima bean dish, with all the time in the world to wait for it, and it comes out as a far more marvelous job than the anxious moment of the rice.

We are all created by our Father. Our Father is a creator; He creates out of nothing. He calls a thing that is not seen as though it were and that which was unseen becomes seen as he keeps the Sabbath.

Learn to keep the Sabbath relative to your children, though you know they are going through hell (or you think they are) and making a mess of themselves. All right, learn to keep the Sabbath, because we are the children of the Most High God, and haven't we gone through a mess? But He, in the depths of our soul, is keeping the Sabbath relative to that which He promised, "you must be born again." We aren't earning it by our creativity, He is keeping that Sabbath relative to us, and no power in the world can spearate us from the love of God.

Read it in the last three verses of Paul's letter to the Romans. "Neither death nor life," and he mentions all the powers man can ever think of . . . "can separate us from the love of God."

WHAT IS MAN?

There is a little poem by Robert Penn Warren. We'll just take the last line of it. He is speaking of the Lord. "He stared into the dark pit of self, whence all had sprung. He said, 'What is man that I should be mindful of him?'"

What is man? It is in you, the individual, that the great things happen. The kingdom of God comes to you, in you. The Davidic tradition has its root and its fulfillment in you. The whole is actually contained within the individual.

We think this whole vast world is so real. Let me tell you, to believe that the visible kingdom is unreal and the invisible kingdom real is the supreme act of faith. To this faith the kingdom of this world has already become the kingdom of our Lord and of His Christ.

The terms Christ, Messiah and Anointed are interchangeable terms. Christ is called the son of God, so is the anointed and so is the Messiah. Let us see who this Messiah is, what He is and where He is. I tell you He is in you. When Paul tells us, "Do you not realize that Jesus Christ is in you, unless of course you fail to meet the test?" he separates Jesus from Christ. He speaks of Jesus as the Lord. But "No one can say Jesus is Lord except by the Holy Spirit." He speaks of Jesus as the Lord and Christ as another. In the Book of Revelations we speak of the Lord and of His Christ.

How are you going to know that Jesus is the father?

He tells you, "I am the Father. He who sees me sees the Father." If he is a father he has a son, at least he has a child.

Let us turn to the Book of Acts. You will find this in the 4th chapter. "O Sovereign God, who made the heaven, the earth and the seas and all within them. Who by the mouth of our father David, thy servant, didst say. Why do the nations rage and why do the peoples imagine vain things against the Lord and His Anointed."

In the King James version of the Bible, that word "anointed" is translated as it should be, "Christ," for the Greek is Christus. ". . . against the Lord and His Christ" not the Lord Jesus Christ, but the Lord Jesus and His son, His Christ. The word translated "servant," ". . . thy servant David," the Greek, for it means "son." What I have just quoted is from the 2nd Psalm.

In the 18th Psalm we find one who also said David is the author. We read: "Great triumphs you give to your king and show steadfast love to your anointed; he is the Messiah, he is the son of God."

Let us turn to this statement concerning the root. "Who is going to open the Bible? Who is going to give it meaning?" We are told in the 5th chapter of Revelations: "He saw the book, but it was sealed with seven seals, and the wise one asks, 'Who can open the book? Who can break the seal?'"

Who is the root of David? Go to the end of the book. Jesus said to the angel, "Say unto John, I am the root and the offspring of David, the bright morning star." He is the root. He is the father of David. He's also the offspring. So the grandfather and the grandson are one in the same being. I am the root and the offspring of David. David remains the son of God.

What is this offspring? It comes out of you. He is buried in you. One day you are going to experience it. Out of your own being will come not another, but you, and you will know you are the father of David, because you'll see him and he'll call you father. You will know he is your son. There will be no uncertainty as to this relationship. It's all buried in man.

"What is man that I should be mindful of him?" These are not the words of scripture but of the poet Robert Penn Warren, for in scripture the psalmist is asking the question, "What is man that thou are mindful of him?" but the poet turned it around and put the words in the mouth of the Lord who said, "Why should I be mindful of man?"

Why? Because the whole is contained in man. This whole venture is already done. It's all in man. The kingdom of the world has already become the kingdom of our Lord and of His Christ because it has been accomplished, and it's being accomplished in the individual one after the other.

It has been fulfilled in me. All that is said in scripture I have experienced in a spiritual sense. But when it came to me it was just as real as this room. It was a cubic reality. There was not a thing gossamer about it, the whole thing was real. One step after the other unfolds itself within the individual and then you know who you are. Scripture began to take on a meaning after the Lion of the tribe of Judah who had conquered, who was the Root of David, discovered David. For only the son can reveal the Father. "No one knows who the son is except the Father, and no one knows who the Father is except the son and anyone to whom the son chooses to reveal Him."

You have been taught to believe that Jesus is the son of God. You have been taught to believe that Jesus Christ is like a title, like a surname Jesus Christ. It isn't so at all. It is the Lord Jesus and His Christ who is the son of God. Christ is the son of God, and the son of God is David. That Davidic tradition is buried in you, individually, and you are going to fulfill it to the very end.

All the kingdoms of the earth will vanish and leave not a trace behind them, for this everlasting divine history is all contained within man. God Himself is buried in man. In the Old Testament He is called Jehovah; in the New He is called Jesus, but this is the same being buried in man and

His son is with Him. The whole drama is a relationship
between Father and son, and one day you will find Him.

If the whole vast world rose in opposition it would
make no difference to me, for I am speaking from experience. I am not theorizing, I am not speculating, I'm telling
you exactly what I have experienced.

The day will come when that which is now imprisoned
within you will be set free. Your body will be split in two
from top to bottom and the spirit that has been held
captive through the ages will be set free. When He is set
free He ascends like a fiery serpent.

The ancient teachers in the second century of the
Christian world spoke of this being, the Christ in man, as
the "suffering servant" and also the "serpent in the wilderness." You will find it in the works of the second century.
The serpent in the wilderness was called the savior and if
one looked upon it he was saved. You don't look upon it,
you experience it.

When he opened the eyes of the blind he said, "What
do you see?" They answered "I see men, but they look
like trees walking." That's a perfect vision. If you saw a
man minus the skin as you see them on a chart, you would
see all the great nerves and nerve centers of the body, the
blood vessels, veins, arteries, all anchored in the brain and
turned down. You'd see an inverted tree. It looks just like
a tree, but inverted. The day will come when it will be
turned up. The root will remain the same, it's the brain,
but the tree grows up. It's now turned down into generation, but then it will be turned around into regeneration. I
recall my vision of maybe twelve years ago. The man is
now gone from this world. He was second in the Labour
Party when Attle was Prime Minister. I saw him in this
wonderful vision one night. I was with a group of men who
were all turned up. They looked like human stags. Their
antlers growing out of their brain reached up almost to the
sky. He took a branch and placed it on his head, thinking
it would give him the same power they enjoyed. He ran
and jumped and fell flat on his face. He tried again and

again, for he couldn't understand how they could cross a chasm with no difficulty as this enormous power grew, but every time he tried it, he failed, for he was trying to do what everyone in the world tries to do, to do it from without.

All the outer ceremonies, the outer rituals, all the outer degrees that men give each other mean nothing. It doesn't work that way at all. It all comes from within because the whole thing is within. Man is turned around by a complete splitting of the temple, for the curtain of the temple is torn in two from top to bottom. At the base of your spine you are going to see a golden pulsing, liquid light. As you see it you are going to know you are it. You are actually looking at yourself, yet it is formless. You fuse with it, and then you become that fiery serpent, and up you go into the brain, and it vibrates like thunder. Then you are completely turned around. The energies that went down into generation are now turned up into regeneration.

I came through the Palace Hotel lobby soon after that experience. I had not mentioned it to my audience in San Francisco, but I had an appointment with a very great artist who was sitting in the lobby waiting for me. As I came through the door she was writing and scratching like mad on a piece of paper. Then she handed it to me.

She had drawn me, and coming out of my head were the antlers. She said, "Neville, they went beyond the ceiling." (It's a three story ceiling in the lobby of the Palace). "You came through the door and nothing stopped it. You came through, there was no obstruction, yet I saw these things coming out of your head like antlers, coming through the ceiling, and nothing could stop them." Well, I had the experience. I hadn't told it because if you tell these things they say, "Why the man is insane, why go spend your money listening to him?" Yet all these things are true. Here is the story of the 22nd chapter of Isaiah. He is now going to speak of the one who can break the seal. In this chapter, the 22nd and 23rd verses, he speaks of the root of David. He speaks of this one who will re-

ceive a peg. He is going to fasten him sure, a secure fasten-
ing. He is going to hang the key of David on his shoulder,
and that one will rule for a time. He will rule as God. Then
the peg will break and all the burdens of Israel will fall
from his shoulder, but he will have that burden to carry
for awhile.

This night I found a room not quite as large as this, but
square, with one door leading into it. I am seated on the
floor talking to twelve men. I am explaining the world of
God when suddenly one of the twelve jumps up quickly
and leaves the room. I know exactly what he is going to
do. He is going to reveal what he has heard. For I was
speaking of a different kingdom. Not the kingdom of this
world, but the kingdom of God, implying, naturally, that I
am king. It's a kingdom, it's a realm, and you are king.

He leaves quickly and had no sooner gone through the
door when a handsome man about 6'6" entered, beautifully arrayed in the finest clothes. He wore the purples and
all the lovely things of the first century. He comes through
the door walking like a soldier straight as an arrow, and
goes to the extreme end of the room. He turns at a right
angle and walks to the end, again the same military turn
walking now to the center. He comes down the center and
stops in front of me.

He was such an important character that as he entered
the room the twelve of us rose and stood at attention. He
came in front of me and as he did so his attendant handed
him a mallet and a peg. He hammered the peg into my
shoulder, blow after blow. It wasn't painful, but I could
feel every blow. Then he took a very sharp instrument the
attendant handed him and with one quick sweep he severed my sleeve; taking the end of it he pulled it away and
discarded it. It was a beautiful baby blue color. I recall
looking at it and seeing how altogether beautiful it was,
what fine material.

He stretched out his arms and formed the cross, embraced me and kissed me on the right side of my neck, and
I, in turn, kissed him on the right side of his neck. Then

the whole scene dissolved and there is the fulfillment of scripture.

Everyone is going to experience it. Everyone will have the opportunity to exercise that power, to exercise that authority. All will have it because the whole drama is contained within the individual. I am not speaking of you in the plural, I am speaking of you in the singular. That's why I say He is mindful of you, because His whole secret is contained in you. When the whole thing is unfolded you are God the Father, and because He is a father, there is a son, and His son is David and David calls you father.

David is the anointed. "He shows steadfast love to his anointed, to David and his descendants forever." So I am the root and the offspring of David. The root is the graft. You take a bud from the tree of life and graft it onto the tree of knowledge. When the time for it to bear comes, it will bear the fruit of the tree of life, not the tree of knowledge upon which it was grafted. That's what a graft does.

You graft a tree by choosing a good bud, a good graft, and implanting it into the tree. When it grows and bears its fruit, it's not going to bear the fruit of the tree on which it is grafted, but the fruit of the tree from which it was taken. We were all taken from the tree of life, that's Jesus. "I am the resurrection and the life."

Here is the sacrifice, the whole tree, and we are now grafted with the tree of life. We do not differ in any respect from the parent tree when we grow, it's the same strength, the same power, the same wisdom, the same everything that the parent tree has.

Have you ever seen a graft? My mother had wonderful roses. She was passionately fond of roses. I can see my mother now, grafting. That was the one job she wanted to do for herself. The gardeners would clean the yard, dig, fertilize, water, but when it came to the grafting, she wanted to do her own grafts. She would select the graft, select the strong tree that would bear it, and when the graft took, the rose it bore was a rose from the tree from which she took the graft.

You have been grafted, as you are told in the Book of James, "Receive with meekness the implanted word which is able to save your soul." No longer will you be eating of the tree of knowledge which is turned down into generation. When it is completely taken, and the time is ripe, you are going to bear the same fruit as that which is recorded in the gospels concerning Jesus Christ.

We are told in the 52nd chapter of Isaiah, "To whom has the arm of the Lord been revealed? Who will believe our report?" You have to take it on faith.

If a man goes into the desert, the wilderness for forty days and forty nights, he is alone and tempted. An evangelist writes the temptations down in *detail*. How would he know unless he was told? How on earth would anyone know unless they were told by the one who had the experience? How would anyone know the experience of the the descending dove unless told? It's actually told in the Book of Mark (the earliest gospel) that it was seen by him alone. No one saw, or experienced it but the one who had the experience, so he had to tell it.

I have told you the experience. These things happened over a period of time. These things reveal to you who you really are. I could tell you from now until the end of time that you are God. I could tell you that you are the father of David, but I can't really convince you. You have to have the experience, and the experience you will have.

Christ is a witness to the truth of God. I am a witness to the truth of Christ, for Christ is the anointed, and the anointed is David. "I have found David, with my holy oil I have anointed him." There is the Christ child. There is the Christ youth. Forever and forever he plays that part. One day, when you awake, you will know you are the Lord because you are the father of David. You'll never know you are the Lord unless David calls you father. When he calls you father there is no uncertainty as to the relationship. It's like memory returning and the whole thing comes back. *

The memory of the bud was so great it produced the

parent stock. If God is a father and I take from that tree (which is a father) and implant it upon this body that is barren, when the bud takes and grows, I must be a father. I must bear the same flower, the same fruit the tree bore from which I took the graft.

We are all engrafted with the Word of God and will all bear the fruit of God. Then you enter an entirely different world, clothed differently, for flesh and blood cannot inherit the kingdom of God. These bodies cannot function in that world. It's an entirely different body. I call that body heaven, for wherever you are clothed in that body everything is perfect. You could pass through hell and it would cease to be hell while you walk through. It would be transformed in harmony with the perfection that springs within you. You couldn't go anyplace and see anything but perfection because you are perfect. Your body is perfect. It's immortal. It never vanishes, it never withers, it's the immortal you.

One day you will see it. It will come out. When you are clothed in it you feel as though you are clothed in fire and air, and you do not raise a finger to transform anyone. In your presence they are transformed. If they are blind you do nothing, you show no compassion, yet the blind sees in your presence. The deaf hears, the one without an arm sees, the arm comes back and fits the socket. The one without a foot has a new foot fit the socket. Wherever you go everything is made perfect. Not a thing can die in your presence because you are the God of the Living. You are the resurrection and the life.

That's your future. That's your destiny. I'll be long gone, but you'll be telling the story, and those after you will hear it and tell the story. They cannot deny it because time will prove it to be true.

Oh, you can deny it now, in words, but you can't deny it in scripture. Bring me the Bible. If you think you know the Bible let us open it together and I will confirm everything I have told you in scripture. It's all there, but man has been taught a strange lesson, and he is completely

confused with these characters and now sticks one on the
outside and worships it. Don't do it.

In the very end they fell before him and he said, "Rise,
you are a man. I'm a man just like you." He wanted no
worship because in the end, when you awake, you are
God. There is only God in the world, God and His son. His
son is His will. He always does the Father's will.

The day will come you will know he is the witness to
the truth of the son, because you will see the son and
therefore know he does exist. He has been resurrected, and
his name is David. Not *A* David, but *The* David, the only
David. No one has to tell you, there He stands before you.
It's absolutely as I have told you, just as I have described
it.

Now let me give you a short portion of the law. We are
living in a world that really is a psychological world. All
things take place in the imagination of man . . . all things.
So, because they do take place there, let them take place
there first, before you expect to see them on the outside.
Assume you are the man you would like to be. Believe you
are. Try to catch all the feeling that would be yours if it
were true. Give it all the tones and feeling of reality and
then sleep. Go sound asleep in the assumption you are
already the one you want to be. Try that and I assure you,
from my own experience, what you have assumed you are,
you will become. You have already become what you are
because you have assumed you are it.

Everything in the world is just like that. It's all imagination. "All that you behold, though it appears without it is
within, in your own wonderful human imagination, of
which this world of mortality is but a shadow." You bring
everything into this world. Lose it, you can repeat it again.
The reality never disappears, for this is a shadow world.
How would you bring it back? By contemplating the state
and assuming the state once again. Feel that you are now
what you want to be and you bring it right back into your
world. Man thinks it's gone and gone for good, but no,
their eternal forms are forever, they never disappear.

One day you are going to have this experience. When you do you will see man differently. You will see everything differently. When you see it, and you are in control of your own being, you will see the whole vast world is dead, actually dead, and you are the living reality of the world. Everything round about you is frozen as though it is made of clay. Time stands still. Then you release an activity within you that you froze, and everything will be animated and continue to fulfill its purpose. Then you will realize where the animation was. It was all in you. You are the cause of it all.

The poet was right when he changed the words around. "He stared into the dark pit of self whence all has sprung." That's where it springs. It comes out of the self. But now men came out and they are all dead. So he buried Himself, reality in man, and man became a living being. By His presence He turned death into sleep and dreams the dream of life. This is the dream of life. The day will come when the dream will end. When it comes to an end you will awake as the dreamer, and the dreamer is God.

It seems sacreligious, but I am telling you the truth. You are not and never were a little worm. You came down from heaven, for only he can ascend into heaven who came down from heaven. No one has ever ascended who did not descend. You descended.

Read scripture carefully and you will see the pre-existence of the one spoken of in scripture as Jesus and the son Christ. Read the 17th chapter of the Book of John. "Return unto me the glory that was mine before the world was." He's asking for the return of the glory he had with the Father before the world was. "Father, I have accomplished the work thou gavest me to do. Now glorify thou me with thine own self, with that glory which I had with thee before that the world was." Isn't that pre-existence?

In this world its splendor was set aside. Now he asks for the return of that splendor, for he's done the work he came to do. Having finished it, he's returning. Only he could ascend who descended. If you have not descended, you cannot ascend, for no one has ever ascended but he who descended.

I am telling you, you did descend. We all came down together. One man fell, carrying all. He chose us in him before the foundation of the world. If one fell, then we all, in him, fell. One was crucified, all were crucified. We are the ones who hang upon the tree. Are we not told in Acts, "They hanged him upon a tree." Then in Galatians, "He took upon himself a curse because he was hanged upon a tree." It is a perfect tree and when the eye was opened, he saw men like trees walking.

This is where Christ is hanging. He's buried in everyone until you awake, and when you awake, you are the Lord and the Father of Christ. You are the Jesus spoken of. You have a son and his name is David. He is the Christ.

These are the trees on which the Cosmic Christ is crucified, because He became Humanity. Not one little man, but Humanity. Every child born of woman is God crucified. That's where the drama begins. It begins at Golgotha. That's when God became man. Then man becomes God at Bethlehem.

Man reverses that. He thinks the crucifixion comes last. No. It begins the drama. Paul said, "I have been crucified with Christ. Nevertheless I live, yet not I, but Christ lives in me. The life I now live in the flesh I live by faith in the Son of God who loved me and gave Himself for me." Now, he who is united to the Lord becomes one spirit with him. If I have been united with the Lord in a death like His, I shall certainly be united with Him in a resurrection like His.

The resurrection is taking place morning, noon and night, but not everyone is called to tell it. Many a one goes to sleep this night, not to awake here anymore, who possibly had the experience but never had the urge to tell it. But I was called; I was embraced by the Risen Lord and sent; therefore, I have to tell it. Tell it I must and I will. I'm telling it as I have experienced it, not as teachers tell it today. I cannot go along with that. I was raised with that, but then I found it wasn't true. When I had the experiences, I found confirmation of the experience in scripture. "Great triumphs he gives to his king." Then he speaks of his steadfast love, "He shows steadfast love to his anointed, to David and his descendants forever," for you are coming out of humanity.

That which is buried in you is coming out of humanity, and who is it? The Father and son. I am the root and the offspring. The father of David is the root of David and the offspring of David is the grandson of that Father, but they are One. He said, I am the father of David (he calls it root). I am the root, and I am also the offspring.

I am the fruit that is born by reason of being grafted onto humanity. He comes out and you are that being. You are the Lord, or the root of David, for David calls you father and there is no loss of identity, may I tell you. No. Although there is only one body, one spirit, one hope, one Lord, one faith, one baptism, one God and Father of all; still, in spite of that oneness, there is no loss of identity. We are one body, yes, yet you are individualized and you will be individualized forever and forever. Clothed in your glorious body, I'll know you, but this will be like a dream, for we have gone through the experience of the dream of life. We won't carry it with us. We will leave it behind. It was essential to the work that the father had planned for all.

We fell, as told us in the 82nd Psalm, "I say, 'You are gods, all of you, sons of the Most High. Nevertheless, you will die like men and fall as one man, O ye princes.' " So we all fell. One man fell and became fragmented. We are the fragmented being and now we are being gathered together one by one. He calls us, calls us back into the one body, the one spirit.

Then you'll see why God is mindful of you. You are precious in His sight. Not one could be lost, because then something would be missing in the body of God, and He could not allow one to be missing. "Not one in all my holy mountain," said the prophet.

Take it home and dwell upon it. You will find that the things you need badly tonight in the world of Caesar will come. Your Father knows what you need. You dwell upon the spiritual things and the earthly things will come. They'll all come. You don't have to do anything on the outside—not a thing! No special diets, no special ceremonies, rituals . . . I recall when I was a strict, strict vegetarian. I had no liquor, no cigarettes, no nothing. My old friend Abdullah, seeing that I did nothing, said, "You know, Neville, you are so darned good you are good for nothing." What a shock. And he was right. I thought I was so good because I didn't do these things. Yet, my brothers who made a great living doing all these things would send me money. So, I woke up. What am I doing . . . I who thought myself so good depending upon those I thought not good because they eat meat, drink and smoke and have fun. My old friend Ab simply shocked me and I realized that I was simply good for nothing. Then I began to accept things in this world, and I know from experience that eating or not eating . . . smoking or not smoking . . . drinking or not drinking will not commend you to God.

The essential character was accused of being a drunkard. "He is a drunkard and a wine bibber, a glutten and a lover of sinners. Harlots are his friends."

All that is part of what I am teaching, for it's all part of God's world, everything in this world is conceived by God, and someone is playing that part. You conceive something? Someone is playing that part tonight in this world, be it good, bad or indifferent, and all loved by God.

In scripture we read, "Go and marry a harlot." That was the advice coming from the Lord. We are all wedded to the Lord, and, any time we turn from Him, we are a harlot. No matter how so-called sacred our wedding is, "I say I will serve the Lord," and we are told in scripture, "Your maker is your husband, the Lord of hosts is His name, the God of the whole earth He is called." Well, if I go to some other God I have gone awhoring, for there is only one God and His name is I AM.

When I turn to anything outside of God, I am a harlot. Forever and forever His name is I AM—that's the Lord. Who hasn't been a harlot? We have turned, all of us, from the Lord and gone after strange gods. Then we are idolaters and to be one who worships a false god is to be a harlot.

Question: In the scriptures, we are told that none will be lost but the son of perdition. Please tell us who the son of perdition is.

Answer: The son of perdition is the belief in loss. The only thing that can die or cease to exist in this world is that which has no right to live or exist. It's not a man. I'll tell you who it is.

Every moment of time you are feeding two beings of which you are totally unaware. Your every evil thought goes to feed one and your every loving thought goes to feed the other. The day will come you will confront them both at the same time. One is an angelic, beautiful creature. The other is the most monstrous thing you ever saw . . . it's covered all over with hair and has a gutteral, human voice.

When I looked at it, it was looking at this beautiful creation, this angelic being, calling her mother, and I struck him. He gloated, for he loved it. He feeds on violence. Then I realized this thing came out of me. I am its father. The angelic being came out of me, so I am her father.

Then I said to myself (for there was no one present but myself), "I will redeem you if it takes me eternity," and that whole thing got smaller and smaller, and in a matter of moments it was gone, and I felt a glow of strength, and she began to glow like the sun. She feeds on my every lovely thought and he fed on my every ignoble thought. He whispered in my ears my ignoble acts because he feeds on violence. If He could cause me to do anything of which I would be ashamed, it would fatten him. If he could only whisper in me to hit someone, that would fatten him and strengthen him. That was misspent energy.

Every lovely, noble thought I have ever entertained feeds her. So I know from experience that's the only thing that dies and it's man's creation. But man does not see it until a certain point in his unfoldment, when he has the strength to face it. It's his dweller on the threshold. It's ever with him. It never leaves him. It goes to bed with him and it whispers into his ear the unlovely thoughts which it needs for its own existence. But when you confront it, you well up with a compassion you didn't know you possessed. You pledge yourself, "I will redeem you if it takes me eternity," and it melts before you, and its energy goes back to you, for energy cannot be lost. Not one little drop of it, if you can speak of it in drops. Nothing is lost. It all comes back. Good night.

IMAGINATION BEGETS THE EVENT

Biblical faith is essentially faith in God as Savior, but this God of whom the Bible speaks is your own Wonderful Human Imagination. Your imagination is God, the immortal you, that is the divine body, Jesus.

Imagination is not some vague essence; it is a person. That person is Jesus in you as your own Wonderful Human Imagination. It is this being in you that must be raised.

Last week I read an article in Time Magazine. When Joseph Chamberlain Wilson was presenting his product, he said, "A strong imagination begets the event." This is his story.

In 1946, at the age of thirty-six, he inherited his father's business and became President of the Halloid Company which made photo copies. The war was over, and the large orders were beginning to be cut back, and he began to look for something else.

A friend suggested he look into an invention which had come out in the thirties but was never commercialized. It was offered to IBM and they turned it down. Offered to Kodak and they turned it down. He took it home, looked it over and found much in its favor.

For the next twelve years he simply imagined and lived in the end. Of course he put money into it. He put all the

127

money he had made in twelve years, plus what he could borrow into it, and invested $75 million towards perfecting the machine. He took stock in lieu of salary and persuaded his executives to do the same thing. In 1960 he brought out the first tangible evidence of his machine . . . the machine is Xerox. He and three hundred odd became millionaires. Today it is $1,700,000,000 a year.

I believe in God not as some vague essence but as a person. I am a person. I do not speak of my imagination as something on the outside I am manipulating. My imagination is my reality.

Man is all imagination, and God is Man and exists in us and we in Him. The eternal body of Man is the Imagination and that is God Himself. The divine body we call the Lord Jesus is buried in these garments of flesh. The true and full awakening of the human imagination is what everyone aches for. My whole concept of life is based upon this concept of God.

I am told, "Do you not realize that Jesus Christ is in you, unless, of course, you fail to meet the test. Test yourselves and see if you are holding to the faith." Do I really believe that Jesus Christ is in me? If I do, I must find out where He is and identify Him.

I have found Him because by Him all things are made . . . good, bad and indifferent. Since He is in me, I must watch what I am doing to catch Him and find out who He is that makes everything in my world. I have found Him to be the dreamer in me that fashions a dream; that being, that's God.

That being, in the twinkle of an eye in the morning, brings me from a deep, deep sleep to the surface mind by building a bridge of incident across which I travel. Only some majestical, magical being could do that. He is the same dreamer that creates my daydreams. The same dreamer that took this man, Joseph Chamberlain Wilson, and this machine which was turned down by the giants and had faith. He had faith in his own imagination. That is the story behind the entire article. You can take any goal in this world if you are willing to be as consistent as he was.

A strong imagination begets the event. You can start now. It's never too late to start if you know who God is. God is your own Wonderful Human Imagination.

I ask you to simply test it. Test to see if you are holding to the faith. If I use the word Jesus Christ, God, Lord or Jehovah, and it conveys the sense of some existent something outside of you, you have failed the test. The Lord God Jehovah is your Imagination and that is Jesus Christ.

Who is the dreamer in the Bible? His name is Joseph. Read the 37th chapter of Genesis; it's a beautiful chapter. It begins with the history of the family of Jacob. Jacob wrestled successfully with the Lord and his name was changed from Jacob, which means, "the supplanter," to Israel which means, "the man who rules as God." Not like a god, but *as* God.

Israel loved Joseph more than any other of his children because he was the son of his old age.

Then, Moses changed his name from Joseph to Joshua. Joshua is the Hebraic form of the word Jesus, and Jesus means "Jehovah is salvation," (the root of the word Jesus and Joshua is Yad He Vau). His name is now Joshua, which is Jesus.

He had a dream and when he interpreted the dream, his brothers hated him. Then he had a second dream which he kept to himself, because the sun, the moon and eleven stars bowed before him, which he knew meant his parents and brothers would bow before him as the ruler, for he would be the Lord.

Then we are told that as he approached, the brothers said, "Behold this dreamer cometh." They sold him into slavery. In the New Testament we read the same story, told differently. "Jesus took upon himself the form of a slave and became obedient unto death, even death upon the cross."

This body I wear . . . this is the cross. This is the garment of slavery, the garment of forgetfulness. I became one who completely forgot who I am when I assumed this form of the slave. Who assumed it? The dreamer. Who is the dreamer? Joshua. Who is Joshua? Jesus. Who is Jesus? The Lord God Jehovah, your own Wonderful Human Imagination.

We are told all things are possible to Him, so when Paul speaks of things he believes, listen to him carefully, he is writing his final letter to Timothy. He said, I know *whom* I have believed" . . . not *what,* everyone will tell you what he believes, "I believe this, that and the other." But that's not what Paul said, for that's all theology, all the ceremonies of the outer world. Paul said, "I know *whom* I have believed." (It's a person now.) Turn to Timothy and read, "Follow the pattern of the true words which you have heard from me. Guard the truth which has been entrusted to you by the Holy Spirit who dwells within us."

He dwells within us. He is the Holy One and He is the dreamer, dreaming your life. He waits on you just as indifferently and as swiftly when the will in you is evil as when it is good. It doesn't really matter, for out of Him springs good and evil. Listen to the words in the 45th of Isaiah, "I form the light and I create the darkness. I make weal and I create woe. I the Lord do all these things."

Yes, out of me all things come, be it good, bad or indifferent. Whatever I imagine. Imagine anything, and it's going to come into your world and project itself on the screen of space to bear witness to your own creative power. You are creating it morning, noon and night.

Watch what you are imagining, for that is God in action. As you imagine, so your life is going to be. You want to be other than what you are? You can be if you know who God is, because by Him all things were made and without Him was not anything made that was made.

Here is the secret. This fabulous world of ours is nothing more than the appeasement of hunger. If you know who you are, you can view the world from any state, for these states are purely a means to satisfy this hunger.

What would you like to be in this world? Begin to

imagine as if it were true. Know what you want, then cease wanting it and appropriate it. Begin, now, to imagine it is true. That is subjectively appropriating the objective hope.

I hope it will be true, so I appropriate it subjectively as though it is true. What am I appropriating? The objective hope. To change my world I have to change my imaginal act. Every natural effect in this world has an imaginal act as its cause. It is not caused by things round about you. The imaginal act is the unseen cause that produces everything in your world. The so-called outside causes are all delusions based on your own faulty memory.

If you have a goal you can attain it. You can attain it by the use of your own wonderful human imagination, for that is God and there is no other God. God is a person and the person is your reality. That reality which is immortal is your own wonderful human imagination. If you should drop now, it survives; it's restored to life in a world just like this but not yet awake. It is the Lord Jesus in you who will awake from this dream of life, and, when He awakes, He is God Himself.

Thinking *from* the end is the secret of it all. Always go to the end. We are always imagining ahead of our evidence. The most creative thing in us is to imagine and believe a thing into existence.

We are told in the 4th chapter, the 17th verse of Romans, "God calls things that are not seen as though they were seen, and the unseen becomes seen."

You cannot see with the mortal eye the man you want to be, but you can walk in the assumption that you are that man. How will you know you are walking as that man? Think of your friends. In your mind's eye, let them see you as you are and hear them say, "I knew him when." That would imply you are not the man they formerly knew.

Dare to clothe yourself with the new man and walk as if it were true. That's the way to success.

Shakespeare puts it so beautifully, "It hath been taught us from the primal state that he which is was

wished until he were." Let us become Man and remain
Man until Man becomes God. That's the story. The gods
become men, "male and female made He them," and remain in Man until Man, being all imagination, awakes as
God.

Take the most marvelous concept you can hold of
yourself or a friend . . . dare to assume it . . . walk in that
assumption as though it were true, and though at the
moment your reason denies it and your senses deny it,
persist and it will harden in fact.

This is what the Bible teaches, but we have gone so far
astray with all of the theologies, the ceremonies and ec-
clesiasticism that it's not true religion. That's not what the
Bible teaches if you read it carefully.

The Bible is the story of salvation. In Genesis you read,
"I will tell you the history of the family of Jacob." Then
he tells you how he loved Joseph more than any of his
other children and made him a long, wonderful robe with
sleeves.

One day you will find out why the sleeves. For the
sleeve is severed so the might and the power of the Lord
may be revealed. These things happen after you are born
from above. You are told he made a multicolored garment.
The sleeve that comes off is the most beautiful baby blue.
He, who seems to be the authority, severs it, and then you
know the words, "Who has believed our report and to
whom has the arm of the Lord been revealed?"

Whose arm is being unveiled? The Lord Himself. All
these things add up to your knowledge of God. You will
not find God as something external to yourself, you will
find Him as yourself. You are the Lord, you are God and
there is nothing in the world but God.

If you take this seriously and test it, you will prove it.
Don't say no to it until you try it. If there is evidence for a
thing it doesn't really matter how stupid it seems to be.

I hope you can actually identify yourself with the
dreamer. Come to some identification with this dreamer so
you do not speak of something on the outside. Your own

being is creating the dream . . . the dream of night and this dream of day.

People ask me, "Neville, what is a vision?" I answer, "This is a vision. This is just as much a vision as a vision of the night. My visions of the night have cubic reality just like this, solid, real. This whole vast world is vision."

As Blake said, "You only have to raise imagination to the point of vision and the thing is done. But the nature of visionary fancy, or imagination, is very little known." This is vision, the whole vast world is vision and you are the one creating it all.

This is the dream of life. If you catch yourself dreaming, the chances are you going to awake. But, if you catch yourself dreaming and decide not to wake, you can control the dream and make it come out as you want it. The same thing is true here if you know this is a dream; you can change the nature of the dream by assuming you are what you would like to be, that friends are what you would like them to be, and walk in the assumption it is true. To the degree you are faithful to that assumption, having faith in God, who is your own Wonderful Human Imagination, it will externalize itself in your world.

That is my story to everyone. I would not take back or alter one word. The whole thing has been explained to me in the depths of my own being. I am not speculating or trying to set up some workable philosophy of life.

I am telling you who I know to be God. I will tell you over and over again God is your own Wonderful Human Imagination. All things are possible to God, for all things are possible to your Imagination. Everything you see in this world was first only imagined. This little thing called Xerox was invented by a man called Carlson, back in the thirties. He knew it would work, but he first had to imagine it and then execute it. No one showed any interest until one came with *real* imagination, one who was awake, and saw the reality.

If I began to imagine now and suddenly, before my eyes, comes the reality of what I am imagining, who is going to tell me it isn't real? I can't show it to someone else, but to me it's real, I saw it. Then, if I had interest in business, I would go all out and sell everything I had to prove it to the world.

My father did that. Every morning he would sit in his chair, put his feet up on the arms of another chair and with his eyes partly shut he would see the day as he wanted it to be. He would carry on mental conversations with men he had to meet that day from *his* premises, and brought them to *his* conclusions. My brother Victor does the same thing. It doesn't matter what things look like in the world, he sees it as he wants to see it. Now they have made millions, but millions, in a little tiny place like Barbados. Put him here and he would be in Xerox, because he has a vivid imagination and he knows how to use it.

But, as Blake said, "The nature of visionary fancy, or imagination, is very little understood. Everything I see in my world is vision." The tree is vision. You think it is solid reality? I can bring it before my mind's eye and it is just as solid as this, so I can make everything real.

The Bible is reality from beginning to end, but it is all vision. From Genesis to Revelations the whole thing is vision.

I ask you to test it. You believe in God? Believe in your imagination, for that's God. You are told in the 14th of John, "You believe in God, believe in me also." He is telling you that he and the Father are one. Then he says, "He who sees me sees the Father." You believe in God the Father, believe in me also, for I am your Imagination. Believe in that and you can't go wrong. Believe in the reality of your imaginal acts and they will become facts, every one of them.

THE
EYE
OF GOD

I doubt if there is any subject on which clear thinking is more rare than the imagination. The word itself is made to serve all kinds of ideas, many of them directly opposed to one another. But I hope to convince you that this is the redeeming power in man. This is the power spoken of in the Bible as the second man, "The Lord from heaven." This is the same power personified for us as a man called Christ Jesus. In the ancient text it was called Jacob. There are numberless names in the Bible all leading up and culminating in the grand flower called Christ Jesus.

It may startle you to identify the central figure of the gospels as human imagination, but this is what the ancients intended we should know. Man has misread the gospels, as history and biography and cosmology, and gone asleep to the power within himself.

I bring you the means by which this mighty power in us may be awakened. I call it the art of revision. I take my day and review it in my mind's eye. I start with the first incident in the morning and go through the day. When I come to any scene that displeases me, I stop right there and revise it. I rewrite it. After I have rewritten it so it conforms to my ideal, I experience it in my imagination as though I had experienced it in the flesh. I do it over and over until it takes on the tone of reality.

Experience convinces me that the moment I have re-vised and relived will not recede into my past, it will ad-vance into my future to confront me as I have revised it. If I do not revise that unlovely incident, it, too, will be re-peated in my world, for nothing dies. But I refuse to allow the sun to descend upon my wrath. At the end of a day I never accept as final the facts of the day no matter how factual they are. I never accept them, but revising, I repeal the day and bring about corresponding changes in my outer world.

Not only will this art of revision accomplish my every objective, but as I begin to revise the day it fulfills its great purpose, which is to awaken in me the being that men call Christ Jesus. That, I call my own wonderful human imagi-nation. When it awakens it is the eye of God and it turns inward into the world of thought. There I see that which I believed to exist on the outside really exists within myself, no matter what it is. I then discover that the whole of creation is rooted in me and ends in me as I am rooted in and end in God. From that moment on I find my real purpose in life, simply to do the will of Him that sent me, and the will of Him is this, that all He has given me I shall lose nothing but raise it up again.

What did He give me? He gave me every experience in my life. He gave me you. Every man, woman and child I meet is a gift from my Father, but they feel in me because of my attitude towards society, my attitude towards my-self. When I begin to awaken and the eye opens, I see the whole is myself made visible. Then I must fulfill my real purpose, which is the will of Him that sent me. The will is to raise up those I allowed to descend within me.

Then starts the real art of revision; regardless of the facts of the case or your impressions of the man, it is your duty to lift him up within yourself. When you do, you will discover he was never the cause of your displeasure. If you look at him and you are displeased, look within and you will find the source of the displeasure.

Let me give you a case history to illustrate this point.

A friend of mine in New York City had a violent quarrel with her daughter-in-law and had been ordered out of their home. Her son had said, "Mother, I love you, but if that is Mary's decision, as much as I regret it, it must be my decision also." That was two years ago.

She went home from my meeting and realized that night after night for over two years she had allowed the sun to descend upon her wrath. She thought of this wonderful family that she loved, yet felt ostracized from.

There had been no correspondence in two years. She had sent her grandson at least a dozen gifts, yet not one was ever acknowledged. She knew they had been received, for she had insured many of them. That night she sat down and mentally wrote herself two letters: one from her daughter-in-law, expressing a great kindness for her, saying she had been missed in the home and asking her when she was coming to see them; then she wrote one from her grandson telling her he loved her, thanking her for his birthday present and begging her to come see him soon.

She held these letters in her imaginary hands and read them mentally to herself until they woke in her the feeling of joy because she had heard from her family. For seven nights this lady read these two letters. On the morning of the eighth day she received a letter which contained two letters, one from her grandson and the other from her daughter-in-law. These letters were identical with the letters she had mentally written to herself seven days before.

Where was the estrangement? Where was the conflict? Where was the source of the displeasure that was like a running sore for over two years?

When man's eye is opened he realizes all that he beholds; though it appears without it is within, within his own imagination of which this world of mortality is but a shadow.

When man awakes he realizes that everything he encounters is a part of himself and what he does not now comprehend is related by affinity to some as yet unreal-

ized force in his own being; that he wrote it but has forgotten what he wrote, yet within himself he started the
entire unfolding drama.

Every man and woman in this world can do what that
lady did. It will not take you years to prove it. What I am
telling you may seem to be bordering on insanity, for the
insane believe in the reality of subjective states and the
sane man only believes in what his senses dictate. I tell
you, when you awake you assert the supremacy of imagination and put all things in subjection to it. You never
again bow before the dictates of facts, accepting life on the
basis of the world without; you know your own Wonderful
Human Imagination is God and that is the Lord Jesus
Christ.

In the 18th chapter of John, Jesus is brought before
the embodiment of reason, personified as Pontius Pilate,
who questions him saying, "What is the truth?" Jesus remains silent, refusing to justify any action of his or anything that was done to him, for he knows, "No man
cometh unto me save I call him, and no man takes away
my life. I lay it down myself."

When you awaken to this truth you see nothing in pure
objectivity, but subjectively related to yourself. You are
the source of all the actions that take place within your
world. When the eye opens it knows that what is an idea to
the sleeping man is a fact to the awakened imagination.

I may think of a friend and make some wonderful
concept of him in my mind's eye. When I sleep it seems to
be a wish, purely subjective, then the eye opens and he
stands before me embodying the quality I desired to see
him express. So, what is an idea to sleeping man (the un-
awakened imagination) is an objective reality to awakened
imagination.

This exercise calls for the active, voluntary use of
imagination as against the passive, involuntary acceptance
of appearances. Never accept anything as true and final
unless it conforms to the ideal you desire to embody
within your world. Do exactly what the grandmother did,

but start it now and do it daily. Results may come tomorrow, the day after or a week from now, but I assure you
they will come.

In 1905 Albert Einstein startled the scientific world
with his equation which no one could even test. Yet today
we know the fantastic results of that equation. Man, not
knowing the power of his own imagination, stands startled
at the results of that unlocked energy.

It was Albert Einstein who said, "Imagination is more
important than knowledge." For if man accepts as final
the facts that evidence bears witness to, he will never exercise this God-given means of redemption which is his
imagination.

I ask you to test it. The knowledge of it cannot prove
itself, only the application of that knowledge can prove or
disprove it. I know from experience you cannot disprove
it. Take an objective, a job, some conversation with your
boss, an increase in salary, anything you desire, but apply
it.

A friend of mine in San Francisco is a ship's captain, a
pilot. One day he said to me, "Neville, I am a trained pilot,
a good pilot, and I love the sea. I have traveled all over the
world, yet now they restrict me to certain waters because
of seniority. No matter what argument I give them, the
union is adamant and has closed the book on my request."
I said, "I don't care what they have done, you are transfer-
ring the power that rightfully belongs to God, which is
your own imagination, to the shadow you cast upon the
screen of space.

We are in this room, yet need it remain a room? Can't
you use your imagination to call this a bridge? This is now
a bridge and I am a guest on your ship. You are not in
waters restricted by the union, you are where you desire to
be. Close your eyes and feel the rhythm of the ocean. Tell
me of your joy in first proving this principle and secondly
in being at sea where you want to be."

He is now in Vancouver on a ship bringing a load of

lumber down to Panama, traveling waters legitimately where the union said he could not go.

I am not suggesting we dispense with unions, kings, queens, presidents or generals. Take no one and dethrone him, but do not give him the power that rightfully belongs to God. Sit in the silence and revise the picture within yourself. Hear the man who said, "No, and that's final," say, "Yes," and a door opens.

Call upon this wonderful power within you. Man has completely forgotten this power because he personified it and called it another. Keep your outer comfort, your religion if it gives you pleasure; all these things are like toys for the sleeping man. But I have come to awaken within you that which sees an entirely different world. It sees a world that no sleeping man could ever see. As he awakes he starts to raise within himself every being God gave him, and may I tell you God gave you every man that walks the face of the earth.

Nothing is discarded, everyone in the world must be redeemed. Your individual life is the process by which this redemption is brought to pass. Just because a thing is unpleasant, don't discard it, revise it. Revising it we repeal it, and it projects itself on the screen of space bearing witness to the power within us, which is our own wonderful human imagination.

Blake said it so beautifully, "Rivers, mountains, cities, villages, all are human." When the eye opens you see them in your own bosom. In your own wonderful bosom they all exist and are rooted there. Don't let them fall and remain fallen; lift them up, for the will of my Father is this, that of all He has given me I should lose nothing but raise it up again. I raise it up every time I revise my concept of another and make him conform to the ideal image I myself would like to express in this world. When I do unto him what I would love the world to do unto me, I am lifting him up.

May I tell you what happens to you when you do it? First of all you are turned around within yourself. You no longer see the world in pure objectivity, but subjectively related to yourself. When my eye was first opened I beheld man as the prophet saw him, as a tree walking. Some were only like little antlers of a stag, while others were majestic in their foliage, and all that were really awake were in full bloom. These are the trees in the garden of God.

We are told in the 61st chapter of the Book of Isaiah, "Give beauty for ashes, joy for mourning, the spirit of praise for the spirit of heaviness, that they may become trees of righteousness, plantings to the glory of God."

That is what every man must do, that's revision. I see ashes when the business is gone, it can't be redeemed, conditions are bad and the thing has turned to ash. Put beauty in its place; see customers, healthy customers, healthy in finances, healthy in their attitude towards you, healthy in every sense of the word, loving to shop with you if you are a shopkeeper.

If you are a factory worker, don't see any cause for a lay off; lift it up, put beauty in the place of ashes, for that would be ash if you were laid off with a family to feed. If someone is mourning, put joy in its place; if someone is heavy of spirit, put the spirit of praise in place of the spirit of heaviness.

As you do this and revise the day you turn around, and turning around you turn up. All of the energies that went down when you were sound asleep and really blind now turn up, and you become a tree of righteousness, a planting to the glory of God. I have seen them walking this wonderful earth, which is really the Garden; we have only shut ourselves out by our concept of self, and we have been turned down.

We are told in the Book of Daniel that we were once this glorious tree which was felled to the very base. It formerly sheltered and fed the nations, comforted the birds and animals from the heat of the day. Then a voice from within said, "Let it lie, let it remain as it is, but do not disturb the roots; I will water it with the dew of heaven and it will once more grow again." This time it will consciously grow, knowing what and who it is. In its past it was majestic, but it had no conscious knowledge of its majesty, and I felled it . . . that was the descent of man. Now he will once more spring from within himself and be a tree walking, a glorious, wonderful tree.

To those who are sound asleep this may seem too startling. This may be just as startling as Einstein's equation was. But I tell you I've seen it. Men are destined to be trees in the garden of God. There is a complete metamorphosis taking place like the grub into the butterfly. You don't remain what you appear to be when man is asleep. There is no more glorious picture in the world than to see this living animated human being. Every branch within him is represented by an extension of himself called another. When he lifts the other up, that branch not only comes into leafage, but it blossoms upon the tree of the man who awakens.

The son of God sleeps in man and the only purpose of being is to awaken him. The man of sense is only a casing; it is called the first man. But the first shall be last and the last shall be first. That which comes into being second, like Jacob, takes precedence over his brother Esau who came first. Esau was the man of sense made of skin and hair, and Jacob was the smooth skinned lad. The second one sleeps in every man born of woman and is destined to awaken as the Lord.

The kingdom of heaven is now, this day, on earth. Awaken, revise your day and project a more beautiful picture onto your screen of space.

THE POTTER'S HOUSE

In the Book of Isaiah we read, "O Lord, thou art our Father, we are the clay. Thou art our Potter. We are all the works of thy hand."

Here we see that the Lord, the Father and the Potter are one. The word "potter" as defined in scripture is "imagination, to form a resolution, to determine." In Genesis we read, "Let us make man in our image after our likeness," that is to form a resolution.

In Jeremiah we are told, "Arise and go down to the potter's house and there I will let you hear my words. So I went down to the potter's house, and there he was working at his wheel, and the vessel he was making of clay was spoiled in the potter's hand. But he reworked it into another vessel as it seemed good to the potter to do."

We have just discovered that the potter, who is our father, who is the Lord, is our own Wonderful Human Imagination. He is working with clay. We are told we are the clay.

I stand for a moment and wonder what I am imagining for myself, for that is the Lord Himself, the Father in action. Is my concept of myself what I would like to be? Or is it spoiled? I don't discard it; I simply rework it into another vessel as it seemed good to me (the potter) to do.

Am I living as I would like to live? Do I have an income equal to my needs? Do I have an income to allow me to do what I would like to do, or am I limiting myself based upon what I think I could do? There is no limit based upon the potter's ability to reshape that image.

Will I take the challenge and reshape the vessel, for the vessel is made of clay and we are the clay? Will I now at this very moment change my concept of myself and my concept of those in my world and see them as I would like to see them? Will it work?

Let us look at the definition of the word, "imagination," as given to us by man. Scripture defines it as God the Father, the potter who fashions everything in the world, but we use it so loosely in this world. We are told that "the simple apprehension of corporeal objects, if present, is sense perceived." This is sense perceived: I can see you, and, if you should speak, I can hear you; that is sense perceived. You are present, therefore, that is real, as it were. "If absent, it is imagination;" in other words, it isn't real, it isn't sense perceived.

Now we will take one of the senses, the sense of smell. Since smell is a chemical sense, a contact is necessary for perception. Now I ask you to join with me. Can you smell a rose? There aren't any roses here or in your presence, but can you imagine a rose and smell it? I can; it's so distinct.

If the rose is not here when I smell it, why is its fragrance in the air when it depends upon a chemical contact?

You cannot smell anything in this world without a chemical contact. I go into the kitchen and I smell gas. The stove is not lit, yet I smell gas; it's a chemical contact. Then I notice that the wind blew out the pilot light and now I can light it. But I could smell the gas; that was a chemical contact. If I could not have detected it, I could have become asphyxiated.

There is no rose here, yet I can smell a rose. You say, "What does that mean?" It means so much to me. You can smell money. Money has an odor unlike anything in this world. You can actually take money and smell it. A money bag is more fragrant to the miser than all the flowers in the

world. It's a pleasant odor to him but not to me. I need
money to pay all of the normal expenses in this world, but
it is not a fragrant odor. But I use this principle towards
getting money, towards meeting all of the obligations of
life, for I am obligated as you are.

So I go down to the potter's house. I can sit in a chair;
I can stand at a bar; wherever I am, I am in the potter's
house, for I have found the potter. The potter is my imagination and the potter is my Father, the Lord God Al-
mighty. I don't have to go any place outside of where I
stand to be in the potter's house.

Now I will see what he is working on. I went down to
the potter's house and simply saw what he was doing.
What am I imagining? Is it a good image I am forming of
myself, my friends and the things I love in this world, or
am I critical, simply making a mess of my talent?

I find quite often I am not using it wisely. I tell you
that the worship of God is to use His gifts. That's the only
way you really worship God. He gave you a talent. The
talent is Himself. It comes through the five senses. I may
be denied four of them as many are born minus one, two,
three or maybe four. Most have the sense of touch, but
some are born blind or go blind, some deaf, some lose the
sense of speech, but in my imagination I can use all of
these talents. Physically they may be denied me, but I still
have an open door from within and I can use it from
within. If I am born restricted, I need not have them all
open on the outside, I can still call upon them from within
as I do now to smell the rose.

In New York City, many years ago, I told a story
similar to this and a friend of mine, sitting in the audience,
decided to test it. In the silence she embraced a huge bou-
quet of roses. She lived in the Towers of the Waldorf
Astoria. When she went home that night she detected a
strong odor of roses as she walked down the hall to her
room. As she opened her door, she saw three dozen long
stemmed beauties on her bureau. There was no note, but
the next day she was informed how it happened.

It seems that night the English Speaking Union gave a party for the present queen's mother, Queen Elizabeth.

They had these roses raised for the occasion and at the end of the banquest they wondered what to do with them. Then the head waiter said, "Mrs. Neemier loves flowers, especially roses. Send three dozen up to her room."

So, Mrs. Neemier was given three dozen of these beauties which she certainly did not expect but she thought she would try it. She embraced some roses and then came these beauties into her room.

I have known people who have taken money from their pocket, felt it and yet it was not present. They feel it, smell it and count it too, and it happens just like that.

Man is not completely confined to the garment and the five senses through which contact is made with the world. He has imagination. Imagination is God, that's the potter, that's the Lord, that is our Father. He gave us himself. The only way to truly worship God is to use His gifts.

He actually gave me Himself because I can say "I am" and that's His name. Now I discover He is my imagination. Blake said, "I know of no other Christianity and no other gospel than the liberty both of body and mind to exercise the divine arts of imagination." Then he adds, "The apostles knew of no other gospel."

We are living in a world of imagination. If I say to the average person who believes in God, "The whole vast world was created by God. We are living in a world of God." They will bow and admit to that. But let me say, "The world in which we live is a world of imagination," they say "No, this is real and what you imagine is unreal." Yet everything they tell me is real was once only imagined.

The clothes you wear had to be first imagined. The chairs on which you are seated; the building in which we are now housed; everything first had to be imagined before it was objectified and executed in this world. What is now real to us and seemingly an objective fact was once only imagined. We had to imagine going to the moon before we did it. Everything here was in the potter's hand and that potter is your own wonderful human imagination.

Everything in this world that we call natural has an imaginal cause and not a natural cause. A natural cause only seems. It is a delusion of the perishing memory. That's the one thing that suffers when God became man; he had to completely forget he was God when he became man. Memory faded completely but the reality remained, for He is man's own Wonderful Human Imagination.

Man is all imagination, and God is man and exists in us and we in Him. The eternal body of man is the imagination and that is God Himself. We speak of it in the New Testament as Jesus; that is the divine body of the Lord Jesus, your own wonderful human imagination. He is not on the outside; He is within your own wonderful imagination.

If I should use the word God, the word Lord, the word Jesus, and in any sense whatsoever it causes you to think of some external existing presence, you have not found the true God, the true Lord, the true Jesus. If for one moment you hear the word and out flies the mind toward some external object, either in time or space or both, you haven't found the right Jesus, the right Lord.

You are told, "Do you not realize that Jesus Christ is within you?" Then comes the challenge, "Test yourselves and see whether you are holding to the faith." Well, the minute you hear the word, "Jesus," and you think of something other than your own wonderful human imagination, you have failed the test.

The other day I turned on the TV to see the football game, and as I switched channels I saw this man talking to undoubtedly enormous crowds, praying to an outside Lord Jesus. All this nonsense . . . there is no outside Lord Jesus. When he rises in you, he rises AS you. When he awakes in you, he awakes AS you. When he awakes IN you, he is the Father. You will know he is the Father, for YOU are the Father and confirmation of that comes before you in the form of David. David stands before you and you know exactly who he is and who you are. There is your son bearing witness to the fact that you are the Lord Jesus, you are the Father. This is the story of scripture.

Now I ask you to use your imagination wisely and lovingly first on yourself and then everyone you contact in this world. I don't care who he is, don't discard him, he can be refashioned. Read the story carefully in the 18th chapter of Jeremiah. The word Jeremiah means "Jehovah will rise." He is buried in man. He is man's imagination.

These are the first four verses; "Arise and go down to the potter's house and there I will let you hear my words. So I went down to the potter's house and there he was working at his wheel. And the vessel he was making of clay was spoiled in the potter's hand, and he reworked it into another vessel as it seemed good to the potter to do."

He didn't discard it. Someone may seem beyond repair; don't discard him, test this power . . . this creative power. There is nothing more wonderful in this world or more creative in man than to believe a thing into existence.

The great poet, the late Robert Frost said, "Our founding fathers did not believe in the future, they believed it in." They didn't think about time bringing about democracy; that time would bring about the country you and I love and live in today; they believed it in. They had an idea and it was not anything that Europe had. Europe did not conceive this idea; it died with ancient Greece. We have the most difficult form of government in the world because we have freedom.

But, our founding fathers did not believe in the future; they believed it in. There is nothing more creative in man than to believe something into existence. Do you know what you want? Begin to believe it in as you believe now that you can smell roses.

Believe it in. What would you see if it were true? What would you hear it it were true? Go to the end and dwell in the end as if it were true. When you do it that way, then actually believe in the power of the potter to make it so. All you and I are called upon to do here is to believe it. To believe in the power of the imaginal act. But to try to

change circumstances before we change our imaginal activity is to struggle against the very nature of things. You
can't do it, because the imaginal activity is producing
things and will continue to produce the things related to
that activity. Unless I change the imaginal activity, I can't
change the things, for they only bear witness to my imaginal activity.

Do it regardless of your present circumstances. While
you sleep it is working. While you walk the street thinking
of other things, it is working, for you have set it in motion.
Believe in the imaginal act. Believe it to be a fact and in a
way no one knows it will objectify itself in this world. It
will become a reality. I am telling you this from my own
personal experience.

As a family we have just celebrated our 50th anniver-
sary in business. We started behind the eight ball on borrowed money, but as we are told in the 133rd Psalm,
"Behold how blessed it is when brothers dwell in unity." I
am one of nine brothers and a sister, and we dwelt in
unity. I left home at the age of 17 to come to America and
return only for contacts with the family. But this close
knit family of brothers just celebrated their 50th anniver-
sary. It really is the most fantastic successful story in a
little tiny place like the West Indies.

I will not mention the quantity of money involved, but
when you have a business, and you double your stock and
double your stock and double your stock, and still pay 20
per cent dividend at the end of the year to the stock-
holders, you are in business. We are satisfied, here, if we
get 6 percent. Any company who is offering 8 per cent,
you will find it gobbled up tomorrow morning. But we
have not gone public. It's all owned by our family. We pay
our individual members and I happen to be one of them,
drawing the same amount as those who are there, but I am
one with them and they know it.

I am one spirit (that's the only reality), so I get my 20
per cent, too, of the stock my father gave me, and he gave
me every share he gave them. We all shared equally when

he departed this world. In fact he gave it in 1939 and lived
until 1959, he was so confident that if he ever needed it
we would give it all back to him. He gave it because by law
in the West Indies a man must outlive his gift five years to
avoid taxation. So in '39 when the war broke out and not
knowing the outcome, he gave equal shares of everything
he had to his nine sons and one daughter.

Since that time it's been split and split and split and
still paying its 20 per cent, because we think alike. When
my brother Victor was 19 he had the vision that imagining
creates reality. He saw a building on the main street with a
sign over the marquee, F.M. Roach & Company; but he
saw the words J.N. Goddard and Sons. My father's name
was Joseph N. Goddard.

Every morning when my brother walked to work, he
never passed that building without reading the J.N. Goddard and Sons, and on his way home at night he repeated
the act. Two years later that building was for sale. We had
no money, but a stranger came in the day of the sale and
asked him if he wanted to bid for it. He said, "I have no
money, no collateral." But the stranger said, "I will have
my lawyer bid for it. Pay me back all the money in ten
years at 6 per cent interest and it's yours."

That day we owned the building. We paid him off in
the ten years and turned around eight years ago and sold
that piece of property, which we bought back in 1921 for
$500,000, to the Bank of Nova Scotia for $840,000, and
there is no capital gain in Barbados.

That's how he thinks. That's what he did. He never
waits for one moment, he knows what he wants and he has
the vessel in his hand. His hand is his own mind and he
simply works on it knowing exactly what he wants. He
doesn't care about rumors. What rumor? It doesn't interest
him. What someone else is doing doesn't interest him, he
knows exactly what he wants and he goes blindly on, getting it.

I will give you one little story. He could sense that the
Second World War was coming. We are a little island and

needed all the help we could get, because only ships were coming in and no planes flying, for in those days there were no commercial flights, only ships. He knew the Germans would do exactly what they did on their second encounter and that is to sink all of the ships they could find. Therefore, what would we do for merchandise?

He went out and borrowed lots of money from the bank and filled our warehouses to overflowing. He rented warehouses and filled them. All of the merchandise was not brought in for human consumption but for ships. If you do not understand the law of the sea, you can bring in all kinds of things and put them in storage, and, when ships need their supplies, you simply empty your store houses and no duty is paid on it. It's duty-free merchandise if it goes from the warehouse to the ship. If you bring it in for local consumption, you pay the usual 30 or 33 per cent on merchandise of that nature. But he knew the island would need it.

After the war broke and ships were not coming in but were being sunk, he was filled to overflowing. But you can't carry that enormous stock (far in excess of one million), you need to move the merchandise. So he went to the governor and asked permission to sell the merchandise to the local people who needed it badly. The governor called a conference of all of the great leaders in business and they said, "No, we have him exactly where we want him. He brought in the merchandise to sell to the ships and to ships only will he sell."

Now we were paying 8 per cent a year on a loan of a million dollars for merchandise we couldn't move. So, Victor reminded the governor that his salary was paid by the local merchants and he was one of the largest taxpayers of taxes on the island. Well, the governor didn't like to be reminded of these normal things.

My brother then went out and called in his lawyers and asked for the legal definition of a ship. What is a ship? The lawyers answered, "A ship is that which is seaworthy. That can take off to sea. What you want is can it take off to an island one hundred miles away." "That's all I want to know," said my brother.

The next day he took a huge ad in the paper and itemized all the merchandise. It read, "Anyone who has a thing that floats and is confident he can make an island can come buy this merchandise tax free. Bring only cash." Do you know we emptied all of the warehouses in twenty-four hours?

They came in their little boats that couldn't have gone three yards, but the definition read, ". . . if you have the courage." They simply bought the merchandise, went out to sea, then came back into the island and sold it to the merchants, and the government was robbed of their 33 per cent in taxes.

My brother uses only the potter's mind. He knows who the potter is. He knows who the Lord is. He knows who God the Father is and he knows He is his own Wonderful Human Imagination. That's God. There is no other God. God actually became what we are that we may be as He is.

God is your own Wonderful Human Imagination. Let no one rob you of that and give you a false god. They are always trying to give you a false god. When you see anyone praying to a god on the outside, he has a false god. When he has to go to a certain church to pray he has a false place.

That's not the temple, *you* are the temple of the Living God and the Spirit of God dwells in you. That spirit is your own wonderful human imagination. Now use it wisely, and to use it wisely you use it lovingly. Any time you use your imagination lovingly on behalf of another you are mediating God to that other. Always use it lovingly and you can't go wrong. Things will simply flow and flow in your direction and always in the good.

So while I sleep here, my brothers thousands of miles away, living in unity, are expanding my holdings for me. "Behold what a blessed thing it is when brothers dwell in unity." That's the one thing my father instilled in all of us. He could not bear anyone to say, "He is wearing my tie," my father would remind him that it's not his tie or their tie but all his, for he bought it all. So, in our home we always used to say, "The first one dressed is the best dressed."

If you have a family, try to instill that in them—to be unified as in that 133rd Psalm. "Behold what a blessed thing it is when brothers dwell in unity."

Scripture teaches who God really is, but man doesn't read it carefully. "O Lord thou art our Father, we are the clay and thou art our potter, we are all the works of thy hand." Now, "Rise and go down to the potter's and there I will let you hear my words." Then we see exactly how it's done. He didn't say that because He was the Lord; He wouldn't have a vessel that was spoiled.

Your concept of a man may not be perfect, but that being conceiving is the Lord. Your concept of yourself is not the most perfect concept as it could be, but that being conceiving (which is yourself) is the Lord, that is God; that is the Father. If your concept of yourself is not what you would like to be, don't discard it; simply change it. Change it by feeling yourself to be the man you would like to be. "What would it be like if it were true?"

So often I speak of states of consciousness. Do you know what a state of consciousness is? It's a mood, just a mood. What would the mood be like if it were true? If I were the man I would like to be, what would the feeling (the mood) be like? If it were true, how would I see the world and how would the world see me? That's a mood—that's a state. You enter that state and abide in it; dwell in it and live in it. It may not come tonight or tomorrow morning, but if you remain faithful to that state (to that mood), it will externalize itself in your world and you will move from wherever you are (if you don't like what you are) to where you want to be. It works that way because you know who the potter is and you know where the house is. Wherever you are in this world, that is the potter's house, for you are the temple of the Living God and the Living God is the potter. The potter is your own wonderful human imagination. So now you know who He is.

Let no one lead you astray to a false God, to some other being that doesn't really exist. When you hear the word God, the word Jesus (which is a marvelous word), don't let your mind jump outside to something other than your own wonderful human imagination. Stop and observe what you are imagining and see what you are doing to Jesus.

No one has ever seen Him. There is no description of Him in scripture. Why? You do not observe imagination as you do objects in space. You are the reality which is called imagination, so you can't observe it, you observe the fruits of its activities.

Look at what is happening in your world; you are observing the fruit of our imaginal activity, the activity itself you don't see.

God, the Father, who is the Lord, who is the potter, is like pure imagining in myself. He actually dwells and acts in the depths of my own being, underlying all of my faculties including perception. But he streams into my surface life least disguised in the form of productive fancy. I catch him in the act when I am daydreaming.

I sit down and think of a friend and wonder, what is he or she doing, and then I catch him in the act. That's how you catch him. But you can't see him and you will never really know him until his son stands before you (and his son is David). When David stands before you, there is no uncertainty as to the relationship. Then you know who you are and it's all your own wonderful human imagination.

Now I hope you know who the potter is, and where his house is, and what the vessel is, and what the clay is—and I hope you will take it seriously and try to become the perfect potter. You will not discard vessels that are spoiled but rework them into the more perfect image as it seemed good to the potter to do.

FACTS
OVERFLOW
THE
WORLD

When we read about the flood in the Bible, we think it's an old book describing things that happened unnumbered years ago, but I tell you it's contemporary.

This morning, as is my custom, I turned on station KFAC. All day long it plays lovely classical music you can read to, so I sat down with my Bible and read as I listened. One interruption that came today was an ad from the Herald Examiner. They were advertising this paper as the one paper in our city that gives the facts only with no embellishment.

May I tell you facts have overflowed the world like the flood. Man is drowned with facts, victimized by facts. It is in the imagination that everything lives and not in its fact. Unless imagination penetrates the facts the deluge remains a deluge. We are now in the deluge; this is the flood.

A man is in jail. That is a fact. He knows he is there for X number of years. That is a fact. He waits and hopes that in some strange way he will be released from his confinement and never uses his imagination to penetrate the fact.

In March of 1943 I, too, was imprisoned in the army and I didn't want any part of it. I simply penetrated the fact and saw myself in my apartment with my family. In nine days I was in my apartment in New York City, honorably discharged.

A friend of mine was also in the army. He was a
Freudian, a professional psychoanalyst. When I wrote him
in detail exactly what I did he didn't answer my letter. In
New York City he used to come to my meetings. One day
he said to me, "I come to your meetings, Neville, because
you turn my daily bread into the substance of faery and I
like that. But when I listen to you, I hold the chair and put
my feet firmly on the ground to feel the reality and the
profundity of things, as you weave your story concerning
moving off in one's imagination." He would not penetrate
the fact, so when did he get out? Years later when the
other millions did, for he simply could not let go of the
facts.

This is the flood and there is no other. We are drowned
with facts, victimized by them. Does the Bible teach the
story of getting through the facts by using your imagination? It certainly does. Let me take you into the 27th
chapter of the Book of Genesis, the Book of the Beginning.

If you are not familiar with the story of Isaac and his
two sons (they were twins), let me refresh your memory.
It is said that Isaac was the father of two sons, Esau and
Jacob. Esau was the hairy one, he came out first, and
Jacob, completely hairless, came out second and sup-
planted the other. Now we are told that when Isaac was
old, his eye was dim so he could not see. In other words he
was blind. He said to his son Esau, "I cannot see and my
days are numbered; go into the fields and hunt, then bring
me some well prepared, tasty venison."

We are told that Rebecca, who loved her second son
more than she did the first, overheard the conversation
between Esau and his father, and, because she wanted
Jacob to get the blessing, suggested they take one of the
kids from the flock and kill it. Jacob said, "Suppose my
father discovers it?" Then his mother said, "Leave that to
me. It will be on my shoulder if he discovers it." Then
wrapping himself in the skins of the kid, Jacob went
quickly into the presence of his father who said, "Come

near that I may feel you, my son, to know whether you are really my son Esau or not."

So Jacob came near Isaac, his father, who felt him. Then Isaac said, "The voice is Jacob's voice but the hands are the hands of Esau," and he gave him his blessing. He had no sooner left the presence of his father when Esau came in with his savory venison. The father said, "Who was it that came, for I have already eaten?" Then he discovered it was his son Jacob who came with guile and betrayed him. "But," said the father, "I have given him your blessing and I cannot retract it, and blessed he is, all will serve him."

In the earlier passage of this same book we are told about the ark. Build the ark with three decks, the lower, the second and the third deck. Now you may think of it as a huge building, but use your imagination and you can't conceive of any building that could house all of the animals in pairs, and all the so-called "good" ones to be in seven pairs, and enough food to feed them for forty days and forty nights. Nevertheless that's the story.

But there are three decks: the obvious facts, a psychological interpretation of these so-called facts, and then the spiritual consummation of the stories making the lower, the second, and then the third deck.

Here is a perfect example of the second deck. This room is a fact, but suppose I don't want to be here. Suppose it has become a prison to me, can I get out of it? I can if I know how to penetrate the fact. If I know that I am the ark, that all things exist in the human imagination and the human imagination and God are one, in my imagination I can penetrate any wall. Right now, in the twinkle of an eye, I can stand on the street and see this podium without a man standing before it.

You may say, "What will that do?" Let me do it and feel the solidity of the street under my feet; see this building from the street rather than looking at the street from here, and I will be compelled to go there.

This is what scripture teaches, that is my blessing. I can penetrate a fact and penetrating a fact I can stand wherever I want to stand in this world. Then the promise is made, "Wherever the sole of your foot shall stand, that I have given to you." I am not going to make you a promise and not fulfill it; I will give it to you if you can stand upon it.

When I was in the army I actually stood on the floor of my apartment, felt my bed and all the furniture in the room giving it reality. But my friend wouldn't allow himself to sleep in one place and assume he was sleeping elsewhere, because, to him, that was a divided state of mind and he didn't want to become a split personality; he wanted to be completely coordinated. He was coordinated all right, for the next three years . . . all in one little spot in his barracks.

Benjamin Disraeli once said, "Man is not the creature of circumstances, circumstances are the creatures of men." He knew how to create things all in his imagination. Scripture is not secular history; it is contemporary. It didn't happen thousands of years ago; the flood is on, the whole vast world is inundated with facts.

Don't condemn anyone. Jesus didn't condemn the woman taken in adultery but asked, "What do you want? Go and sin no more." He didn't call the act of adultery a sin, but if you call it a sin, don't do it. Sin is simply knowing what to do and not doing it. If I discover what to do to penetrate a fact and do not do it, I have sinned, for I have an unfulfilled desire. But if I go beyond the fact, create a condition for myself and dwell in it, thinking *from* it instead of thinking *of* it, it MUST appear in my world.

The great fallacy of the world is perpetual construction, deferred occupancy. In my mind's eye I can create all the lovely things I would like to realize but never occupy them, if I do not penetrate the state and give it cubic reality.

The sense of touch is something we believe in more profoundly than the sense of sight, hearing or smell. I stumbled upon this one day in a dream. In my dream I came upon a huge pillar driven into the ocean. The brace it formerly supported was gone but the piles remained. I knew I was dreaming so I said to myself, "If I hold this pile until it seems solidly real I will comply myself to awake." I held the pile with all of my might and then said, "Neville, you know you are dreaming now, awake," and I awoke in the water. I am actually holding that pile, standing in water in what I formerly knew to be a dream, but now I am in a world just as real as this. I realized I was in a very primitive area in the East Indies. Then a strange looking animal came down toward the beach and I became panicky, and at that moment of shaking emotion I awoke on my bed in New York City. From that experience I discovered the secret of feeling.

So Isaac said, "Come close, come near that I may *feel* you my son." He heard the voice and said, "Your voice is the voice of Jacob. Come near that I may *feel* if you are really Esau." He did it by feeling.

Many years ago while lying on my bed in Beverly Hills, I became aware I was seeing what I shouldn't see. I was looking at the interior of a plush hotel. Consciousness followed vision and I found myself in the room. But I knew I was on the bed so I went back to bed. Still seeing the interior of the room I returned and came back again. I must have done it twenty times it was such fun. I would enter the room and it was just as real as this room, and then I would return to my bed.

Finally I said, "Regardless of the consequences, I am going to explore." So I went into the room. From the bed it appeared to be about 30 x 20, but when I entered it with the decision to explore, the room closed in on me and became a third of itself, about 10 x 7, and I found it to be a dressing room of a large suite, beautifully done but not occupied.

I desired to go through the door, but not like something gossamer. I opened it with my hand and walked through, for I was solidly real to myself. Then I walked down the hall which intersected the main corridor. All of the lights were on and two ladies were walking toward me.

Now I knew this began as a dream and I knew all ends
run true to origin, so if the origin is a dream this is a
dream. I said to the ladies, "This is a dream. This whole
vast world is a dream." They were afraid of me. Well, who
wouldn't be afraid of a man who walks up to you and tells
you this whole vast world is a dream? They got just as far
as they could from me and walked right next to the wall,
duck-style, one behind the other looking at me very sus-
piciously.

Then I saw an object hanging from space. It reminded
me of a similar light fixture I had seen in a friend's home,
so I said to them. "Look, see this?" Then I held it and to
my surprise it wasn't gossamer, it wasn't memory image, it
was solid, it was real. Well, they took one last look at me
and darted into the main room.

Here I am standing alone holding onto this fixture. I
said to myself, "Neville, you know this is a dream. The
origin is a dream; therefore, the end is a dream. Come on,
wake up." I closed my eyes to the obvious, held the fixture, opened my eyes again and I'm still standing there.

How am I going to get back to my room in Beverly
Hills? There was no place I could go to take me back, but I
remembered feeling is the secret, so I imagined my head
was on a pillow. When I could feel a pillow under my head
I suddenly felt myself in a horizontal position. I could feel
the pillow but I was cataleptic; I couldn't open my eyes,
move a hand, move a finger. I am a living being in a dead
body.

I said to myself. "They will find the body tomorrow
morning, and because I am insured, to prove nobody took
my life, they will have to cut it up to find out why I died."
They always have to ask that question, and, even if they
can't find the answer, they'll give it a name anyway.

I couldn't open my eyes but in about fifteen or twenty
seconds, with great effort, I could move my little finger,
then my hand. We were sleeping in a double bed, so I
pushed my left hand out and felt the warmth of my wife's
body. At that I knew I was back on my bed. In another

fifteen or twenty seconds, with great effort, I opened my
eyes and everything in the room returned to consciousness.
Now I stepped into a world just as real as this. I am
telling you there are worlds within worlds within worlds,
and they are all here right now. It's just like turning on a
radio. You turn it ever so slightly and you have a new wave
length and a new station bringing something entirely
different, yet they are not interfering with each other.

These worlds are all here, now, and they are peopled
just as we are peopling this world, and they are just as real
as this. It's terrestrial. I seemed to walk into it, but the
same area permeated the bed, and the bed did not obstruct
it, and that world into which I stepped did not obstruct
the house where I lived in Beverly Hills.

I tell you, the facts are the flood. That's the deluge.
There was no other flood. We are actually inundated with
the facts of life and we change them everyday. Today this
is the cause of so and so, tomorrow it's another cause and
the next day still another. We believe these causes to be
facts and we worship facts.

All things are in the human imagination. Man is all
imagination, and God is man and exists in us and we in
him. The eternal body of man is the imagination and that
is God Himself. There is no other God. It's all your own
wonderful human imagination. The one thing the whole
vast world aches for is the awakening of the imagination.

When imagination is awakened within you, you are set
free from the horrors which we call the world of nature.
For nature is simply that principle on which depends the
sameness of form in transmitted life.

Haven't you observed that at a certain time of the year
money is tight? Why? It's a habit; it's a transmitted state.
You fix the fact in your mind's eye that money is always
tight in the month of December, and, if you received fifty
thousand today, you will loan the money out or give it
away before December goes by, so you will be tight again.
It's a peculiar slavery, this thing called nature, in the sameness of forms in transmitted life.

Now you can penetrate the fact and break it. I come
not to abolish the law and the prophets but to fulfill them
and tell you the *real* law. It's not washing your hands
before meals although that's a very nice, clean thing to do.
It's not certain diets, doing this, that or the other. Jesus
explains the entire law as psychological.

He takes one of the commandments, which is a graphic
one, to show you how everything must be interpreted
psychologically. He said, "You have heard it said of old,
you shall not commit adultery. But I say unto you any
man who looks lustfully upon a woman has already committed the act *in his heart* with her." What man has not
violated that? So he tells you the whole thing is psychological.

You can't restrain the impulse, maybe you are afraid
of the consequences. Maybe you are afraid someone will
find out. There are many fears, but the impulse was there
and he tells you the impulse was the act. If the impulse
was the act, then creative acts are imaginal, for it was an
imaginal act. I must observe my imaginal acts, for the
imaginal act will become a fact and confront me.

A lady in San Francisco once said to me, "I think my
brother is innocent but I do not know the facts of the
case. He was given six months of hard labor in the army
and I don't think he deserves it." I said, "You want him
out?" She said, "Certainly I do." I said, "If he was out
where would he go?" She said, "He would come straight to
my place." "If he came to your place, what would you
do?" She answered, "I would throw my arms around him
and kiss him. I would feel him." I said, "All right, when
you go home tonight, imagine your brother is there, throw
your arms around him and hug him."

The next Sunday morning in my meeting in San Francisco that woman rose and told this story. "I went home
and imagined I heard the doorbell ring, I ran downstairs,
flung open the door and there stood my brother. I had
done it so vividly I went back upstairs disappointed
because I hadn't actually seen him standing there.

A few days later I was sitting in my room when the doorbell rang. I almost broke my neck to get downstairs, because I knew what was going to happen. I threw open the door and there was my brother."

The secret is to practice. We are the operant power and the flood is on. Let no one tell you the flood is over. The flood is deeper and deeper because we want the facts of life. You want the fact? Then you make the prison walls all the thicker.

Learn how to penetrate the facts. If you penetrate the fact you must go to a certain objective beyond the fact. What do you want now? Go into the state of the wish fulfilled. What state? The state *you* decide. Determine what you want in this world and go right into that state; then ignore the facts.

Suppose the facts still deny what you did. It doesn't matter, let the facts remain, they will all dissolve if you remain faithful and occupy the state.

You can do it with a job. A friend of mine in New York was an engineer. One day he said, "Neville, I want more money and more responsibility. I want to work for a certain firm." I said, "Do you know where they are?" He said, "Yes, they are on Madison Avenue. They build bridges and dams all over the world. I would like a job where they would send me overseas because then I would get three times the salary." I said, "Before they would send you overseas you would work in the home office first, wouldn't you? Then go to the place and see where you would sit if you got the job."

He walked into the place, picked out the desk, familiarized himself with the surroundings and then went home. At home he assumed he was seated at that desk, working for that company at the salary he wanted. Within a month he had that job and two weeks later he was on his way to the Near East to build bridges.

Now, the inevitable day will come when you will take off this garment. When that day arrives you will find yourself instantly restored, in a terrestrial world with problems

you have here, but you'll know how to solve them because
you know the principle.

The whole Bible from beginning to end is contemporary. Jesus is not something that died; he's something that
lives within man. He is dwelling in man. God Himself came
and comes into human history in the person of Jesus in
you, in me, in everyone in the world. The day will come
you will know you are the Lord Jesus. Now you are asleep,
but the day will come when you will be completely awake
to the fact you are the Father.

You could have all the power in the world and yet not
know you are God. You could have a sense of awareness
that there is not a thing in the world but yourself and yet
not feel you are God. If you had power to destroy the
universe you still wouldn't know you are God. But when
His Son comes, and you know you are his father, then you
know you are God. There is no other way to know it.

In 1926, about ten o'clock in the evening I was reading
a book. It fell upon my chest, and I awoke the next
morning about nine and had not turned from left to right
in the entire interval, because the book was still on my
chest and the light still on by my bed. Usually, in the
course of a night, a man turns often from side to side. But
I went into a deep, deep sleep and in that state I became
infinite light. There was no circumference, I was the center
of it all and there was no other light outside of me.

No sun, no moon, no stars but nothing outside of
being that infinite, pulsing light, but still I did not bring
back the feeling of being God. But when I saw His son and
that son called me Father and I knew I was his Father,
then there was no doubt in my mind as to who I am. One
day you will experience it and then you will know that
you are God. Not a thing in the world will convince you
outside of that.

But in the meanwhile learn to penetrate the facts. A
man imprisoned need not be behind bars; we are imprisoned by gluttony. He can break it if he knows what he
wants. Maybe he doesn't really want to break it. But if he

does, let him create in his mind's eye a simple scene where he is telling a friend about how he has no longing for food anymore. He didn't take any drugs; the longing just isn't there anymore.

All things are acquired. Today I like an oyster, especially those lovely Eastern oysters, but the first time I ate an oyster I could have died. I was a small boy about nine or ten when I went to the Virgin Islands with my mother. We went to a boarding house where we all sat at a big table. Mother told me to watch and do whatever the lady did. Well, I sat down at the table and here was a plate of oysters. I had never seen an oyster in my life before.

I saw this lady take a little fork from the side of her plate, so I picked up my fork. Then she took a little horseradish, a little tabasco and mixed them together, dipped the oyster into the mixture, put it in her mouth and ate it as though she had honey in her mouth. I expected the same so I did as she had done, and when I got that thing in my mouth, Lord, it wouldn't go down, I could bring it up (I'm not supposed to, mother had told me that), so there it stuck. But the funny thing about it,. I not only had that one, I looked down to find five others and they had to go down.

You don't come into the world with these tastes, you acquire them. You can acquire the taste for living in comfort. You can acquire the taste of living as a gentleman, as a lady. You want to live like a gentleman, like a lady with no pressure to pay the rent; all right, assume you are that gentleman, that lady. Penetrate the facts. The facts tell you you are not. Penetrate the facts and live in the state as though you had it and may I tell you from experience you will.

Don't ask me how, the ways and means are contained within the state you enter. You enter a state and it contains all that is necessary to externalize it. Pick out a lovely state, go right into it and dwell there. I call that occupying the state and thinking *from* it instead of thinking *of* it. Just as you now think from your present state where all the facts surround you to anchor you into it, get into another state all in your imagination and the facts will appear to anchor you there.

You know when you move into a new home or a new city you have to adjust yourself to it? Well, you are the pilgrim passing through unnumbered states. The states remain, but you, the pilgrim, pass through them. Like a traveler, pass through it. Poverty remains a state when a man who was once poor moves out of it into the state of affluence, but he doesn't destroy the state of poverty. Anyone can fall into it.

Blake said, "I do not consider the just or the unjust to be in a supreme state but only to be in states of sleep which the soul may fall into in its deadly dreams of good and evil." It toys with a state, finds itself enamored with it and falls into it. He is not supreme because he is wealthy and another ignored because he is poor; these are states. Don't condemn the occupant of the state, for the occupant is God.

The occupant in a state called poverty is saying, "I am," before he says, "poor." He doesn't say, "I am poor," meaning he is different, as far as "I am" goes, from the one who says, "I am rich." It's the same I AM-ness that occupies the state of poverty as is occupying the state of wealth. You can go into any state and the being in the state is God. You wear these states as you wear your clothes.

But you must be consistent and *believe* it. You are told in the 6th chapter of John, "We believe and have come to know that thou art the Holy One of God." First, faith adventures on a possibility, then something steadier than faith appears, personal experience. "We believe and have come to know . . ." I first had to believe and then venture on my belief; that was the faith. After that comes personal experience.

I ask you not to be like my friend who said he always came to my meetings because they turned his daily bread into faery, but always held onto the chair and put his feet on the floor to keep his sense of the reality and the profundity of things. If I turn your daily bread into the substance of faery, all well and good. The whole vast world is going to vanish anyway, but you, the reality, you can't vanish.

You came here to experience. This is a school of educative darkness. You came here to test the being you are and the day will come when you will awaken to who you are. That's what every man aches for, the awakening of the imagination.

It comes and you have the sign of the awakening when the child is born. The minute that child is born the great burden of nature is broken because now you are free.

The Bible is contemporary, it's something that is forever and forever. Some may believe the flood is a myth, but you know what the flood really is, it's the facts of life. This is what has overflowed and overflowed and drowned man, victimized man because man is the ark and all things exist in man's imagination . . . everything.

Let things disappear from here; they are, in reality, in you. Everything is in your imagination, so it's all contemporary and you can make it alive again if you want to.

THREE PROPOSITIONS

My first proposition is this: The individual state of consciousness determines the conditions and circumstances of life. The second is: Man can select the state of consciousness with which he desires to be identified; and third: Man can be what he wants to be.

If the first proposition is true that the individual's state of consciousness is the sole cause of the phenomena of his life, then the normal, natural question is asked, "Why doesn't he change it to a more desirable state?" That is not as easy as it appears.

I hope to give you a technique to make it easier, but man finds it hard to leave the things to which he has grown accustomed. We are all stuck in the habitual.

It may seem strange, but a very sordid cartoon appeared in the "New Yorker" during the last war; you might have seen it, it was one by George Price. In it you see a single little room, a sink piled high with unwashed dishes, plaster falling from the walls, and these two middle-aged people, she sitting on a chair, disheveled, matted hair, and he with torn clothes, his feet stuck upon the table, with socks exposing holes. She is reading a letter from their soldier son abroad. The caption of the picture was this: "He says he's homesick." You should have seen the interior of this house . . . one room, completely disheveled, but the lad was homesick! Man finds it difficult to detach himself from the habitual.

It is the height of folly to expect changes to come about by the mere passage of time, for that which requires a state of consciousness to produce its effect could not be effected without such a state. If I must be conscious of the thing I am seeking before I find it, then the only thing to do is to acquire that state of consciousness.

A state of consciousness is the sum total of all a man believes, accepts and consents to as true. It need not be true, it could be false, a half truth, a lie, a superstition or a prejudice, but the sum total of a man's beliefs constitutes his state of consciousness. It is the house in which he abides. As long as he remains in that house, similar problems will confront him and the circumstances of his life will remain the same. He may move physically, but he will encounter similar conditions because he can't get away from the house in which he abides.

The Bible speaks of these houses as mansions of the Lord, as cities, rooms, upper rooms; all kinds of words are used to describe individual states of awareness. The appeal in the Bible is to move out and occupy the upper story, meaning to move up to a higher level within one's self.

If you do not know the state in which you abide, here is a very simple technique you may employ to discover it. Listen within yourself and observe your internal mental conversations, for the state is singing its own song and it reveals itself in man's inner speech. If you will listen attentively and uncritically to what you are saying inwardly you will discover the state. Then it will not surprise you that things are as they are, for you will hear within yourself the cause of the phenomena of life.

What you are inwardly saying and doing is far more important than what you outwardly know or express. When you know what you are doing inwardly, you can change it. If you have never uncritically observed your reactions to life, if you are totally unaware of your subjective behavior, then you are unaware of the cause of the things in your world. But if you become aware of the state, then you simply go about changing it.

Man stands forever in the presence of an infinite and eternal energy from which all things proceed, but it follows definite patterns. It doesn't move out of man and crystallize in some strange haphazard manner; it follows a definite track. The track it follows is laid down by the man himself in his own internal conversations.

Man is called upon to change his thinking that he may change his world. We are told, "Be ye transformed by the renewal of your mind." Man cannot change his thinking unless he changes his ideas, for he thinks from his ideas. If I would change and become transformed, I must lay new tracks, and the tracks I lay are always laid down in my own internal conversation.

I can sit in a chair, stand here or walk the streets, yet I can't stop talking. Man does not realize he is talking because he is never still long enough to listen to the voice speaking within himself. But inwardly he is whispering what is taking place as conditions and circumstances in his world.

Most of the things he whispers are negative in justifying his behavior. There is no need to justify. He is excusing delay or failure, arguing, judging harshly or condemning. Man has a peculiar, strange feeling, a little affection for the feeling of being unwanted or being hurt, and he likes to talk about it. Try to get out of this habitual state.

It can be just as difficult as trying to keep that soldier boy away from that sordid room; he goes back into the sordid rooms within himself. You don't see unwashed dishes within yourself, but if you could only see the internal psychological state in which most of us abide, you would see a room far dirtier than the one George Price illustrated in the "New Yorker" magazine. They are all unwashed plates within us. We wash them on the outside, but we are told in the Bible, we leave the inside unwashed and become whited sepulchres.

If I sincerely desire to change my world there is no one

I need to change but myself. I don't need to change you as
an individual, but I do need to change my attitude towards
you. If you dislike me, or I think you do, the cause is not
in you and your behavior but within myself. If I search
honestly I will find that when I think of you it is never a
pleasant conversation I carry on. Let me now sit down,
bring you before my mind's eye and imagine a conversation which would imply a radical change in my world. Let
me change my attitude relative to you by laying new
tracks.

This energy, which is only thinking, moving across the
tracks laid down in my own inner conversations, will result
in changes in my outer world. If I repeat the conversations,
doing it often, it becomes a habit. Then I will find that
while I am about my Father's business in the outer world,
I am inwardly, through habit, carrying on these changed
and livelier conversations.

Now, a transformation of consciousness will definitely
result in a change of environment and conditions. But I
mean transformation of consciousness, not just a slight
alteration like a change of mood. It is nice to change a
mood, but I want a trasformation. By transformation I
mean when the state into which I have moved becomes a
habit and grows stable, it expels from my consciousness all
of its rivals. Then that central habitual state defines my
character and constitutes my new world.

But if I only do it a little bit and return to my former
state, then, although I might have had a temporary lift, I
will not notice radical changes in my outer world. I will
only notice these changes if inwardly I have truly changed.
Then without effort on my part I will find the outer world
changing to correspond to the changes which took place
within me.

I can't stress this too often; I can't give it too great an
importance; this wonderful thing called man's ability to
talk within himself. Without the aid of anyone in the
world, sitting alone at home you can construct a sentence
which would imply the fulfillment of your ideal. You can

construct a sentence which would imply that a friend has realized her objective. What would she say to you if she had it? Listen attentively and if you are still enough you will hear as coming from without what really you are whispering from within yourself. Man is this wonderful temple in which all the work takes place, and the outer world is only a projection of the work done within.

We are told in the second chapter of Genesis that Adam was placed in a profound sleep. There is no reference where he awoke as Adam, but as the second man called Christ Jesus. All men sleep in Adam and awake in Christ.

A man who is totally unaware of the mental activity going on within him is the one who sleeps as Adam. He may walk with his eyes wide open, be very important in the world, wealthy, famous, have all the things you admire, but if he is totally unaware of that mental activity which is the cause of the phenomena of his life, he is sound asleep and personified as Adam. He will read his Bible and think it is a literal story, that Adam was put to sleep and a rib taken from him to form a woman called Eve.

But when man begins to awake he realizes this symbolical Eve is only his own emanation now called by the name of nature. Nature is his slave and must fashion life about him as he fashions it within himself.

If man is asleep he fashions it in confusion, but he fashions it anyway, for he uses the very technique his Father used to build the world. He uses his mind and his speech. But in the state of sleep he brings about strange conditions and doesn't know he's the cause of the things round about him. As he begins to awake, he awakes as Christ Jesus, and the being personified in our Gospels as Christ Jesus is simply the awakened, loving imagination.

Imagination love is incapable of hearing anything but the lovely. When that being begins to awake in you, you don't see things in pure objectivity anymore, you see everything subjectively related to yourself. You never meet a stranger. You may meet a man for the first time, but you know he is not really a stranger, for the man had no power to come into your world save you drew him in.

"No man comes unto me save I call him." "No man takes away my life; I lay it down myself." "You didn't choose me, I have chosen you." In that state you become incapable of hurt, you've overcome all the violence you formerly expressed in the world. You feel no condemnation for the sleeping man; he is dreaming confusion because he doesn't know who he is.

Take this technique and try it consciously. I am not appealing to the passive mind that passively surrenders to appearances; I am appealing to the Christ in you which is the active conscious use of your own wonderful human imagination. When you sit down and predetermine what you want to hear, listen until you hear it, and refuse to hear anything other than that, you are using the one power in the world that awakens man. You are using your own wonderful human imagination, and that is God Himself.

A lady wrote me a letter this past week. Her husband had called her, and he was very upset because his company had a contract for six hundred feet of film to be delivered to Chicago in less than twelve hours. The film had been developed by Acme, returned to them when they discovered only three hundred feet was good. The other three hundred feet was totally blank.

She hung up the phone and sat in the silence until she heard, within herself, the phone ringing. Picking it up with her imaginary hands, she heard the tender loving voice of her husband explaining that the whole thing had been resolved; they had found what seemingly they had lost forever. She listened until her whole body became still in hearing only what she wanted to hear. An hour and ten minutes later, while still in the silence, the phone rang. It was her husband calling to say that Acme had found the missing three hundred feet of film and the whole thing was perfect.

She liberated herself by listening until she heard

exactly what she wanted to hear. Then she heard it one hour and ten minutes later. Now the majority of people would not have acted upon it; through habit they would have gone into a stew; they would have fumed and fretted, and that very day had he brought home the negative news that undoubtedly he would have, they both would have slept allowing the sun to descend upon their wrath.

Last night did you allow the sun to descend upon your wrath? Did you sleep with any trouble, any vexation unresolved? Or did you go to bed having resolved every vexation and trouble of the day. Did you rewrite the play? If you didn't, then you heard, but you aren't a doer.

You are told in the Bible, "Would that ye be doers of the word and not mere hearers only. For if you are a hearer and not a doer, then you are like a man who sees his face in the mirror and turns and straightway forgets what manner of man he is. But if you are a doer and not a forgetful hearer, then you shall be blessed with the deed, for you will look into the law of liberty and you will liberate yourself. Liberating yourself you shall be blessed with the deed." You will find that story in the first chapter of the Epistle of James.

Believe these propositions and, having believed them, do something about it. Go out and apply what I have told you concerning inner speech; it is truly the greatest of the arts. Listen and only hear what you want to hear. Take your imaginary hand and put it into the imaginary hand of a friend and congratulate him on his good fortune. If you want one to congratulate you, allow yourself to be congratulated. Don't bend your head, hold it high and accept the congratulations.

That is truly entering the kingdom of heaven, for the kingdom is known by a loving, knowing communion. You can enter the kingdom at every moment of time, ride the street car, ride the bus, and with all the talking and gossiping, you can enter the kingdom and bless a friend by just imagining the friend is with you, and you are putting your hand in his congratulating him on the good news you've heard concerning him. Then listen as though he answered in kind. In that moment you have blessed him. He may be a thousand miles away, but from that moment on things will begin to stir within his world, for you have brought about a change within the structure of his mind, and every modification of the structure of a man's mind must result in corresponding outer changes.

THE
TRUE
LIFE
OF MAN

The true life of every man is God within him. God is becoming more and more a fact by personal experience. You can speculate about God and speak of Him as an impersonal force, an oversoul and all the other things that men throughout the centuries have done, but eventually you will discover that God is a person. You will discover He is not external to yourself, for you will discover that you are God. That is the mystery.

All scripture was written from the inward mystery and not with a mystical sense put into it. The Bible has no reference at all to any person that ever existed or any event that ever took place or occurred upon earth. But man throughout the centuries has mistakenly taken personifications for persons, the allegory for history, the vehicle that conveyed the instruction for the instuction, and the gross first sense for the ultimate sense intended. These characters are personifications of the eternal states of consciousness.

When we speak of Abraham, we are not speaking of a man; we are speaking of that foundation stone of consciousness that starts civilization. Paul tells us quite clearly in his letter to the Galatians, "I am a Jew of the seed of Abraham, of the tribe of Benjamin." He never denied this

foundation of himself, yet he tells us that the story of
Abraham and Sarah is an allegory. Then he interprets the
story for us.

Abraham had two sons, one by a slave and one by a
free woman. The one by a slave leads us all into slavery.
The woman was Hagar, a slave in Sarah's houshold. Then
he speaks of Sarah and calls her the Jerusalem from above.
She is our mother who leads us into freedom, into liberty.

Abraham is the foundation of all, the father of all
nations, and the story is an allegory. If the origin is an
allegory, then the end must be an allegory, yet it is the
truest story ever told. Scripture is not secular history; it is
eternally true, but it's written from the inward mystery
and not with some mystical sense put into it.

Paul said, "He has made known unto us the mystery of
His will according to His purpose which He set forth in
Christ, as a plan for the fullness of time to unite all things
to Him. Things in heaven and things on earth. In the end,
there is only God."

We read in Genesis, "And God said, let us make man in
our image." Look up the word "make" in Strong's Concor-
dance and you will see you could have used the word
"become." It's the same word in Hebrew. You could have
said, "And God said, let us become man in our image."
Now you have an entirely different picture.

In becoming man, He forgot He was God. He can't
pretend He is man. Eternity exists and all things in eternity
independent of creation which was an act of mercy. That
act of mercy was to take that which was dead and turn
death into sleep. The dreamer in man is God. The dreamer
in you is your own wonderful human imagination. That is
God.

"All things were made by Him and without Him was
not anything made that was made." Who did it? Your own
wonderful human imagination. God said, "Let us . . ."—
that's plural—"Let us become man," and we foresaw
what would happen if we became man. The 82nd Psalm is
considered by all scholars to be the most difficult to in-

terpret. The head of the Encyclopedia Biblica, Thomas Chaney, said it was the most difficult of the 150 Psalms to interpret, and he only hoped that his guesses were not too far off the mark because the first and sixth verses stumped him.

Here is the first verse: "God has taken his place in the divine council, in the midst of the gods he holds judgment." Now the word translated God and gods is the same word, Elohim. In the first, it's singular . . . "God has taken His place in the divine council," but used in the plural, "in the midst of the gods he holds judgment."

Now we go to the sixth verse where he passes judgment on the gods. He said, "I say you are gods, all of you, sons of the Most High, neverthless you will die like men and fall as one man, O princes." The same word—Elohim.

We are the gods who came down as one man fragmented into the unnumbered beings called men. We have completely forgotten we are God. The purpose is to rise as God the Father.

The true life of every man is God within him. God becoming more and more a fact by personal experience. I can tell you from now until the end of time that you are God. You may believe me but you do not know it as a fact until it happens in you. The day is coming when you will have the personal experience of knowing you are God the Father. When it happens, it's like memory returning.

The greatest sacrifice you gave up was your loss of memory. You suffer from total amnesia and do not know who you are. I could quote the 46th Psalm and tell you to "Be still and know that I am God." You could be very, very still and have wonderful things happen within you, like all the dark convolutions of the brain grow luminous and golden clouds radiate from your head; it still would not convince you that you are God.

You can become so still you are infinite light and still not know you are God, though God is defined in scripture as the light of the world. You could become the light of the world and still not have the conviction you are God.

You could have all the power in the world and still not know you are God.

But certain things will happen to you to prove you are not what you appear to be. You are wearing a garment called man and man is dead. You took death upon yourself, which is man, and turned death into sleep. You became an animated soul, believing itself to be distinct in itself and completely independent of everything round about it. It knows nothing of the one who occupies it, who is its very breath, for that one has forgotten who he is.

One day, you will have this experience and then you will know man is not what he appears to be. You will arrest an activity within yourself and everything round about you will stand still. You can stop time. Time is a facility for changes in experience, as space is a facility for experience. But time is a facility for *changes,* for all changes take time.

What appears to be instantaneous isn't really; if there is a change, it took time, no matter how small. But, you can still time. Actually make it stand still. You will find nothing is independent of your perception of it.

Everything stands still. If you placed a piece of raw meat on the equator at midday and arrested time, a thousand years or a million years from that moment, the meat would be just as fresh as the moment time was arrested. It could not decay so there could not be any change.

You are going to have this experience; I have had it on many occasions. Coming into a simple environment and noticing people round about me, I arrest an activity. I feel within my own head and everything stands still. Not one thing can move. The bird flying, flies not. Now a bird in flight, if arrested, would fall by the law of gravity. A leaf may have wind supporting it, but don't tell me a bird in flight, arrested, could stand perfectly still without motion and not fall. Yet, here is a bird in flight and it can't move. The leaves falling, fell not. All things round about me moved not. The diners dining, dined not. Everything stood still.

When I released the activity in me (not in them) they continued on their course as they intended. Now I could have changed their intention when I had them completely still, and when I released it they would have felt they initiated the change within themselves. They would be totally unaware that anything happened external to themselves causing the change. They simply had a change of heart.

Just imagine coming into that power. That is the power spoken of in scripture: "Remain in Jerusalem until you are clothed with power from above." When Paul speaks of Christ as the "power of God and the wisdom of God," that's what he is speaking of.

Not power locked in an atom. Not power locked in a great bomb that can destroy a city, no, that's little firecrackers. That's nothing compared to this power. You could actually empty a city without destroying one brick by stilling the humanity of that city, change its motivation and march the people into the sea, and they would all be like the lemmings thinking that they went to drown themselves and go right in voluntarily. That's the power. But no one will come into possession of it until he awakens as God who is love. Just imagine what he would do if he were not aware that he is God and God is Love.

Can you see the destruction if that power was in the hands of a Hitler or a Stalin? Can't you conceive of the horror in the world if such power could be put in the hand of a monster? One day Stalin will become God and so will Hitler, because God is in them. It's the same God, for God is not divided.

We are told, "The will of God will not turn back until He has executed and accomplished the intents of His mind. In the later days you will understand it perfectly. When you understand it, it is because you have reached the point we celebrate as something external to ourselves called Christmas.

In fact, Paul calls upon us not to observe any day. He said, "I'm afraid that I have labored over you in vain, for I see that you are observing days and months and seasons and years." There is no need to observe any day, for it could happen any moment in time, and when it happens, you awake. Where do you awake? In some little manger out in the Near East? No, you awake within your own skull where you were buried when the decision was made, "Let us become man."

We became men, that men may become as we are. Who are we? We are the Sons of God and when we rise to the height, we are God the Father, for it takes all to become that one which is God the Father. Everyone will have the experience of being God the Father.

But the power of which I just spoke still will not convince you that you are God the Father. Infinite light will not convince you (although He is defined as the Light). Nothing will convince you you are God the Father but His Son, and His Son is not the one the churches teach called Jesus. Jesus is the Lord. Jesus is the Father. The Son of David. That Son will reveal you as God the Father.

One day you will see him and you will know who he is. As you know who he is, you instantly know who you are, for he is your son and he is God's son and God only has one son. We are the Sons of God who form God. The gods become men and play all the parts men are capable of playing—the chief, the judge, the doctor, the fool, every part in the world. At the very end He awakes and resurrects within the grave of Himself.

For, God Himself entered death's door with those who enter, and He lays down in the grave with them in visions of eternity until they awake and see the linen clothes that the women had woven for them. What linen clothes? This fleshy garment my mother wove for me. I will see it when I come out of my skull. I'll see myself in the symbolism of scripture as the child bearing witness to the fact that I was born from above.

Then comes the revelation of my son. He and he alone can convince me I am God. Nothing in the world could convince me I am God. Nothing in the world could con-

vince me that I am but my son who is the son of God. We
are told in the 8th of John, "You will die in your sins
unless you believe that I am He." Then he said, "Only the
Son can set you free and if the son sets you free, you are
free indeed."

This is not a new teaching. Christianity was from the
beginning of the human race but it was concealed within
Judaism. It is the flower of Judaism. Everyone of us must
be Jew, and eventually everyone without giving up Judaism must be a Christian, for Christianity is the fulfillment
of Judaism. I can be a Jew and not be a Christian, but I
can't be a Christian and not be a Jew. If I bear apples, then
I must be an apple tree. I could be an apple tree and not
bear apples.

I can't possibly be a Christian and not be a Jew, but I
can be a Jew and not be a Christian. Because when I am a
Christian in the true sense of the world, I have reached the
end and he has called me Father.

No one is a Christian because he attends some little
church or because someone threw a little water on his head
and called him one who is baptized in the name of the
Lord. You are baptized when you are embraced by the
God of Love. Your bodies fuse and you become one Body,
one Spirit, one Lord, one God and Father of all. That is
your baptismal moment.

You stand in the presence of Infinite Love. He asks
you to name the greatest thing in the world. You answer in
the words of Paul, "Faith, hope and love, these three, but
the greatest of these is love." At that moment He embraces
you and you become one with Infinite Love. Then He
sends you. At that moment of fusion you are fused forever, so you are one with the sender. But in the office of
the sent you are inferior to yourself the sender, so you can
say in the 14th of John, "I and my Father are one, but my
Father is greater than I."

In the office of the one that is sent, naturally you are
inferior to your essential being, the sender who is God the
Father, to whom you will return when you take off the

garment for the last time. For now the journey is over; you have borne the burden the allotted time.

Then will come the splitting of the curtain of the temple. It is man who is the temple of God; therefore, it is the curtain of *that* temple that is torn from top to bottom. "Ye are the temple of God and the Spirit of God dwells in you, a temple not made with hands." When it's torn, the spirit trapped is set free and the rank that was yours as the Son of God is now raised to the higher level of God the Father.

God has a will as told us in Jeremiah and the word Jeremiah means "Jehovah will rise." He will eventually rise in you, as you. "The will of God will not turn back until he has executed and accomplished the intents of his mind. In the latter days you will understand it clearly."

The latter days are the days when you split the great womb which is now the tomb in which you are buried. When you split it, you come out as one being born from above and then you are God, for God is Spirit and it's Spirit being born.

You are going to experience the power of which I speak and I can't tell you the thrill when you feel it. All the people you see seem so completely independent of your perception of them, yet you know they are not. You arrest an activity in yourself (not in them, don't concern yourself with them) and as your head jells, everything stands still. As you observe them, they look as though they were made of clay. Completely dead. Not one can breathe; it can't move; it's only fixed forever.

Then you know that if you release yourself stilled, they would move. You release it and the bird continues towards the bough that was its intention. The waitress now continues toward the table. You see everything animated once more and then you realize the power is in you and not on the outside at all.

You can actually take time and make it stand still. People can't conceive of time standing still, but when you have the vision, you know that eternity exists and all things in eternity independent of creation which was an act of mercy. He took death and turned it into sleep; then He became the dreamer in that garment of death, assuming full responsibility for it, and lost all consciousness of who he really is; he doesn't know he is God.

In one state of consciousness he believes he is a judge and passes judgment on someone who is really God, for there is nothing but God in the world. The one who murders and the one who is murdered, both are God. In the end there will only be God and then we will know that great Shammah, the great confession of faith of Israel, "Hear, O Israel, the Lord, our God, the Lord is one." This one, also is a compound unity—one made up of others, made up of many.

When you see this in the original manuscript they take the last letter of the first word, shama, and the last letter of the last word (both are capitalized), put them together and they form the word witness. You will witness to the Oneness of God, in time. Eventually, you will realize there is no other, there is only God. You are going to know it by your own personal experience.

The *real* you, the true being that you are is God within you. This God becomes more and more a fact by personal experience. At the very end the dove descends upon your hand, called the hand of Noah, and you bring him into the ark. Then you will realize you are the ark and that wonderful image called the dove is true. You will bring it straight to yourself. The dove will rest upon you and smother you with profound love and you will know the drama is over. Here is the seal of approval of the Holy Spirit, for He descends upon him in the form of a dove. Who descends? The Holy Spirit.

The imagery of scripture is perfect, but it's not what the world is taught to believe. The characters did not live as people. These characters are only states of consciousness through which the immortal You must pass.

You get into a state called a thief and you are a thief. But you can get out of that state and move into another state. The state remains like the city remains when the pilgrim moves on. You blame a man because of the state he is in and you think the man is at fault. No, it's because he fell into a state either wittingly or unwittingly. Most of us fall into it because we are sound asleep and do not realize how easy it is to fall into a state.

You can fall into the state of want and remain in that state for all of your earthly days. May I tell you no one is going to make an effort to get you out. You can stay in that state and eat worms for the rest of your days, but if you know the truth, you can get out.

How do I get out of the state? By contemplating what the feeling would be like if I were the man that I would like to be. How would I feel if it were true? If I could only assume the feeling of the wish fulfilled and give that assumption all the tones of reality, all the sensory vividness that I can muster. Then persist in that assumption and it will become natural to me, and after a little while I will find myself returning to it constantly. That state to which I most often return constitutes my dwelling place. If I return to the state often in a course of a day, I will find myself easily living in that state. It becomes a habit just as it is a habit to be in whatever state I am in now.

This is what is called in scripture forgiveness of sins. It tests man's ability to enter into and partake of the opposite. The man who is steeped in want, can he actually feel himself affluent and so feel it that it becomes natural to him? That tests man's ability to enter into and partake of the nature of the opposite. That is forgiveness of sins. I forgive the man for the state in which he fell. I take him out and put him into another state.

He may go back to it. Then the question is asked, "How often must I forgive my brother, Lord?" The brother could be yourself, you know, for here is a sense man. We are riding this donkey of senses. How often must I forgive myself when I find myself going back into the old state? Seventy times seven.

Don't take seventy and multiply it times seven, but

rather as long as it takes me to persuade myself that I am
the man I want to be. I may do it the first time. It may
take me a day, a week, a month to persuade myself I am
that which I am now assuming I am. At the moment
reason denies it and my senses deny it, but can I persist in
that assumption until it becomes natural? If I do, it has to
externalize itself, for the power is within me; it's not on
the outside.

I only have one thing to tell you and that is what I
have discovered from my own personal experience of the
greatest book in the world . . . scripture. Scripture is my
biography, as it is your biography. The day will come you
will experience your biography and you will know the God
spoken of in scripture. You are the God spoken of. You
are the one who is a father and you have a son to bear
witness to fatherhood. Your son appears and there is no
uncertainty as to the relationship. You know exactly who
he is; he knows who you are. Then you know for the first
time you really are God.

Though you are limited because you are still wearing
the garment and still forgetful of the being that you are,
you can't forget that experience. The wisdom and the
power that is yours comes only when you take off the
garment for the last time. Then you ascend to where you
were before you came down, because "No one can ascend
into heaven but he who descended." You could never in
eternity go into heaven unless you first descended from
heaven, and you can't get there until you are born from
above. "Unless a man is born from above, he cannot in any
wise enter the kingdom of heaven."

You are born from above and you come out of the
grave. The grave is a womb, your own wonderful skull,
that is your tomb which forms itself into a womb and you
come out. Not as a little infant, it's only the sign of *your*
birth. You are born and the infant comes wrapped in swaddling clothes to bear witness to the fact that you are born
from above. Then comes all the other signs, one after the
other, and in a very short span of forty-two months the

whole drama is over. You are left here in the garment with the memory of what happened, to tell it to anyone who will hear it.

Paul tells us in Colossians, "The gospel that I have preached to you was preached to everyone under heaven." Can you believe that? We know this much, in the first century a very small percentage of civilized man lived in the Mediterranean. We had the vast Orient, the vast parts of Europe where they were running around in leopard skins and never heard this, so how are you going to take that statement?

It is right, for in his letter to the Galatians he tells us that, "The scripture, foreseeing that God would justify the heathen" (or gentile, it's the same word in Hebrew) "preached the gospel beforehand to Abraham." If you take it as a historical event, Abraham preceded this letter by two thousand years. If he is the father of all and he chose us in him before the world was, in preaching it to Abraham, he preached it to me.

If you take it in a state of consciousness in which all were contained, then we all heard the story of God's plan of redemption. He prepared a way for His sons to return. They are now in the world of death because they are wearing garments called men. But, you will have the power to stop time. This is what you are headed towards. Everyone is going to have it. Not one Son can fail to return as the Father.

If this does not interest you today, it's perfectly all right. He said, "I will send a famine upon the land. It will not be a hunger for bread or a thirst for water but for the hearing of the Word of God." When that hunger comes, nothing can divert you, but nothing. You have to find out the secret of that Word of God.

Let me remind you. All scripture was written from the inward mystery and not with a mystical sense put into it. We give them names but they are all states of consciousness.

Although we speak of them as we do of Shakespeare,

where did all of these characters of Shakespeare live, save in the mind of Shakespeare? But we quote the character, forgetting Shakespeare did it.

A friend of mine came to our home many years ago when they were showing a series of the Kings of Shakespeare on television. She is a very ardent British subject born in Canada and feels that anything that comes out of the British land must be perfect. She sat on the couch with me as we watched TV. As these wonderful words came out of the mouth of Richard III, she said, "You see, these men were wonderful, cultured gentlemen and not what the people think." I said, "Look, dear, that was Shakespeare. Richard III could not even read or write those sorts of words. Shakespeare wrote it."

Then she said, "Oh yes, yes," but it wasn't one minute before she slipped right back into that state of consciousness and again repeated, "You see how wonderful they were!" I said, "My dear, that's Shakespeare." I repeated that all through the evening and still couldn't convince her at the end that these kings did not originate these thoughts. It all took place in the mind of Shakespeare, just as all this takes place in the mind of God the Father.

It's like one grand brain and we are brain cells in the mind of the Dreamer. He is dreaming it all, but in the end He individualizes us, His sons, as Himself and not one will be lost, not one in all my holy mountain, as He told us in Isaiah. "Call my sons from afar and my daughters from the end of the earth." Call them all, for not one can be lost.

MIND
& SPEECH

The whole manifested world goes to show us what use we have made of God's gift. Receiving a gift does not mean that we are going to use it wisely. But, everyone has the gift and the world simply reflects the use of that gift.

In the "Merchant of Venice," Shakespeare puts these words into the mouth of Portia. "If to do were as easy as to know what were good to do, chapels had been churches and poor men's cottages prince's palaces. It is a good divine who follows his own instructions. I can easier teach twenty what were good to be done than to be one of the twenty to follow my own teaching."

You and I have been given a gift. To what use have we put it? There is a book written during the time of the first century (at the time of our gospels) called the Hermetica. This is a translation by Walter Scott. He said, "There are two gifts that God has given to man alone and to no other mortal creature. These two gifts are mind and speech. The gifts of mind and speech are essential and identical with immortality. If they are used rightly, man will not differ in any respect from the immortals. And when he quits the body, these two will be his guides and they will lead him into the troupe of the gods and of the souls who have attained to bliss."

He is not speaking of any outer speech. I am sure this has happened to you, I know it has happened to me many times. You go to a party where there are many people you do not know. You meet them and the usual greeting, "It's nice to know you," "What a joy to know you," "Pleased to meet you," and then you have drinks and your little hors d'ouevres and the party breaks up. Then you hear someone say, "What a creep, what a bore," yet they were so pleased to meet them.

The outer words did not conform whatsoever with what they were really thinking on the inside. And God sees not the outer man; he sees the inner man. It's the inner speech that is frozen in the world about us. The whole vast world is but frozen inner speech. What are we saying on the inside?

We are told in the 50th Psalm, "If a man orders his conversations aright, I will show him the salvation of God." If one could only control these inner conversations morning, noon, and night, and carry them right into the dream world, he would know what world he is creating.

Stop for one moment and ask yourself, "What am I thinking now?" You are carrying on a little tiny inner speech at every moment of time. You may be in the presence of someone who the world thinks important but you don't, and inwardly what are you saying? Only God hears what you are actually saying. Outwardly you are pleased to meet him and flattered with the contact, but inwardly what are you saying?

This is what I ask everyone to observe. Observe what you are actually doing on the inside, for that is what God sees. What you are doing on the inside, you are doing in little tiny speech movements and they are crystallizing in the manifested world round about you.

So, if to do were as easy as to know what were good to do, we all would be kings; we all would be everything we want to be in this world. But we find it more difficult to do than to know what to do. I could tell you from now to the end of time, but only practice will do it, just practice.

A man looks at a building beyond his wildest dream of ever acquiring and he has desires that he does not share with anyone but his mother. She despairs because she knows he could never obtain ownership, but he loves her and shares only with her.

He sees a sign implying that he does own it. Inwardly he is saying, "It is my building," as he reads his own name on that building. Day after day, as he goes by he reads his own name on the building which implies he has it.

Then, two years later, out of the blue, the building is for sale, and a stranger comes in and offers to put the money up to buy it. He had no collateral, but that day he was owner of the building. He conducted the most fantastically successful business for many, many years. Then an offer came to buy the business. He paid $50 thousand for it with another person's money and sold it, without capital gain, for $840 thousand, all by inner speech.

You cannot read something without using your inner speech. No one sees it, but I read something and inwardly I am repeating what I am reading. I saw that on the bus a few months ago as I was going to Beverly Hills. Here was a man reading the paper and every word he read he was forming on his lips. Could I have actually interpreted the motion of the lips, I could have told you exactly what he was reading. Everyone is doing that but not as obvious as he did.

You read something and inwardly you are repeating the words. The thing is all in your imagination (that's all it was in his) . . . only his imagination. That was God's gift. It's translated in the Hermetica as mind. "God has given to man and man alone two gifts and to no other mortal creature. The gifts are mind and speech. These are like the gifts of immortality and by these gifts he does not differ in any respect from the immortals. If he uses them wisely the whole world is his."

Are we not told that the world was created by the word of God and things that are seen were made out of things that are not seen? Out of the nowhere we create by

inner speech and the use of . . . (call it mind if you will)
. . . I like the word imagination. It inflames me. Imagine a
state, any state. If I can only persuade myself of the reality
of the state imagined. That's the important thing. To
believe in the reality of the state imagined.

But to know what to do is not the same as doing it.
For "If to do were as easy as to know what were good to
do, chapels had been churches and poor men's cottages,
prince's palaces." And how many teachers in the world
follow their own instructions? Then he goes on to confess,
"I can easier teach twenty what were good to be done than
to be one of the twenty to follow my own teaching."

Let me make it quite clear. You have the gifts. You
can speak. Even if you are dumb, you can still speak. You
form these little speech movements within yourself. Make
them conform with your wish fulfilled. Do what Robert
Milligan did when he was a poor boy and had nothing but
a brilliant mind. A great, great understanding of literature,
but no money and he was tired of his poverty. Knowing
how the mind works, he constructed a sentence, if true,
then he was no longer poor. His sentence is this, "I have
(not going to have) a lavish, steady, dependable income,
consistent with integrity and mutual benefit."

That was the great Robert Milligan who was the head
of Cal Tech. He gave us his discovery of cosmic rays and,
when he died, left a fortune behind to his charities. I know
the YMCA was one of them.

He lived a full, wonderful, marvelous life. Everyone
who met him benefited from the meeting, yet he started
from scratch using this simple technique. Using the gift of
God that God gave to every person in this world, mind and
speech.

Whether you be a Frenchman, an American or any
other nationality, you have speech and you have a mind.
Instead of accepting what you have already done with that
gift, ignore it, you brought it into being. All this is solidi-
fied speech, the whole vast manifested world.

Now turn from it and reconstruct the sentence, as this

one of whom I spoke changed his entire pattern from a poor boy to a fantastically wealthy successful business-man; because he never forgot how to apply the principle.

He was one among those who found it just as easy to DO it as to KNOW it, while others find it easy to KNOW what to do but difficult to do it. I have seen it time and time again when I would say, "Do you not know what you are doing to yourself?" "Yes, but just give me one little moment, for I am so enjoying getting even with them." Getting even with no one, for there is no one else in the world.

You are told in Isaiah 45, "I am the Lord and beside me there is no God." Now you want the word? He said, "The word is very near unto you. It is in your mouth and in your heart that you can do it. See, I set before you this day life and good, blessings and curse, death and evil. Choose life that you and your descendants may live."

The whole thing is before you. You can choose death if you want to because the word is in your tongue. It is on your mouth; it is in your heart and you can do it now. You don't have to ask who will go up to heaven and bring it down for me or go into the depths and bring it up for me. It is now, nearer than you know. It is in your mouth and in your heart and you can do it now. What would you do? What sentence would imply that you are now what you would like to be? You know what to do. But, it's not knowing *what* to do, it's *doing* it.

Someone got this most marvelous revelation. I was there the morning it happened. "Stop spending your thoughts, your time and your money. Everything in life must be an investment." I so loved it, I incorporated that thought in the chapter "The Coin of Heaven" in my book AWAKENED IMAGINATION. She would be the first to confess that, although it came through her and it was her revelation from God, she never applied it.

I can see her now rushing to the library to learn the meaning of the two words "spending" and "investing." To spend is to put out without hope of return, to waste. To

invest is expecting a return on your equity. There must be
a return on equity. "Stop spending your thoughts, your
time and your money . . ." Time must produce some return; it is precious. Your thought is speech and it must be
invested, not wasted. Everything must be invested and not
wasted.

But, "If to do were as easy as to know what were good
to do . . ." What a marvelous sentence. You'll find it in the
first act, the second scene, put on the lips of the character
Portia. "How difficult for a man who teaches to follow his
own instruction." And he, himself, confessed, "I can easier
teach twenty what were good to be done, than to be one
of the twenty to follow my own teaching."

I ask you to really apply it. Don't think that "knowing" what to do is going to do anything for you. It's the
DOING that matters. If you find yourself carrying on any
negative kind of conversation, break it. Even though it
gives you pleasure. You may think no one heard you. May
I tell you the only One that matters hears you every
moment of time and that's your Father. He sees in the
very depth of your being and knows exactly what you are
doing and builds your world out of these inner conversations.

If you are not satisfied with the world in which you
live, blame no one, but turn within to these two gifts and
use them wisely. We are told to, "Order your life according
to your conversations." Then, in Ephesians 4 we are told,
"Put off the old nature which belongs to the former conversations and put on the new nature."

The new nature is sometimes translated the new man,
the old nature the old man. So, if I equate the old nature
with the former conversation I must equate the new man
with the new conversation. He identifies the inner speech
with man's nature, so what am I actually doing on the
inside of myself? I am doing it morning, noon and night. I
can't stop it. If I stop for one moment, it isn't. You can't
stop it. You take it into dream and you are still talking.

You are inwardly talking every moment in time. What

are you saying? Watch it, be careful what you are saying, because your whole vast world is this inner conversation pushed out, and you can change it only by changing the conversation, because the conversation is equated with your nature.

If you walk the street, ride a bus or sit alone you are still talking. Every moment of time you are talking and all you need to do to find out what you have been saying is look at your world, for your world reflects this inner speech. I am not going to tell you I have not faltered. I would not for one moment tell you I am always in control of the inner conversation. You react. No one heard it, but you heard it and your Father heard it, and you are going to build your world based on exactly what you have done.

Watch it morning, noon and night, for the end of everyone's world is Christ. Everyone is moving towards the fulfillment of being God Himself. Therefore, you are going to play the story of Christ as told in the gospel. When He awakes and unfolds within you, you are Christ and you know you are.

I hope everyone not only listens but believes what I have said. I have told you what I know from experience. God Himself came and comes into human history in the person of Jesus Christ in you, in me, in everyone. But when He comes in you, he awakens AS you. Read the story then. All that is told in that story concerning Jesus Christ you are going to experience.

Then you tell the story to those who will read it and believe it when you feed them with the loaves and the fish based upon the law . . . how to get the building, get money, become famous; they love it. Then you turn and emphasize the end, the promise. And the promise is you will be as God. You don't need buildings because the world is yours and all within it. You don't need anything because the WHOLE is yours, but they can't see that; they want more loaves and more fish.

Watch carefully what you are saying morning, noon and night. When you go to bed watch your inner conversa-

tions and see that the sun is not descending upon your
anger. Resolve it at that very moment and then make it
conform to your wish fulfilled. Make that wish fulfilled a
thing of love. What would it be like if it were true? Then
carry on a conversation from the premise of the wish fulfilled, all clothed in love, and watch how things happen in
your world.

If that is your last thought, it will dominate the dream
of the night. Your Father is speaking to you constantly
through the medium of dream and vision. Then you'll see
the whole thing unfolding within you and you will know
you are the Lord Jesus Christ. You don't go out and
scream it from the housetops; you know it and walk in the
comfort of being the awakened man who is God.

Let everyone say what they want to about you but pay
no attention to it, because they have to do it as the separation must take place. Don't justify it. Self-justification is
the voice of hell. And don't try to always be right.
Another almost incurable disease of man is the necessity of
always being right. Don't make any effort to prove you are
right. You know what you have experienced and you can't
deny the experience, so you go your way telling it just as it
comes to you and it comes in the most glorious manner.
It's all in scripture.

When the truth comes into the world, he comes not to
bring peace but a sword. He is going to separate you from
that traditional background that enslaved you in the past,
because real progress in this world, religious progress, is a
gradual transition from a God of tradition to a God of
experience. For you experience God and the whole thing
reflects it. His son calls you father and there is no uncertainty as to who he is and who you are. Your memory
returns when you stand before your everlasting son. He
knows it and you know it. No person in the world could,
in any way, dissuade you from knowing this, for you have
experienced it. You can't deny it.

I am telling you what's in store for you. Use the gift
wisely. Start now to use it, for if you do, you are told, "I

will show you the salvation of God." Read it in the very
last verse of the 50th Psalm.

They translate the word "conversation" to " manner
of life," and some "the way of life," but in the King James
times that phrase is used and it's always "conversation."
"Put off the former conversation and then be renewed in
the spirit of your mind." You put it off, I have to replace
it with something, A new conversation. You put it off; it's
equated with the old man. Now, as I put it off, I have to
replace it with something. A new conversation. You are
told in the Book of Joel 3:10, "Let the weak say I AM
strong, for there is no other God. I AM the Lord and
besides me there is no other God."

You make the choice. You can choose life or death.
Good or evil, a blessing or a curse, it's entirely up to you.
Look into this manifested world and see what we have
chosen, when every morning the headlines are nothing but
disaster. Either the newspaper men feel they must print it
to sell papers or else we, ourselves, are demanding it from
them. Every morning, noon and night we feast upon this
unloveliness and carry on these little internal mental conversations with ourselves. But they don't remain there.
They balloon and objectify themselves and become solidi-
fied as our manifested world.

This whole manifested world goes to show us what use
or misuse we have made of God's gift. And God's gift is
your mind and your speech. It is not your outer speech,
for we know how deceptive that is. God sees only the
inside. Man sees the outer appearance and God sees the
inner man.

When you watch your inner conversations, you are
actually watching your new nature. If you don't like it,
change it and take off the old man and put on the new
man, and he will show you the salvation of God, and then
the whole thing will unfold within you.

I tell you from my own experience, before the promise
was realized in me, inwardly, I would argue with my
brother mentally. We were five thousand miles apart and I

needed money. When I found myself arguing with him, I broke it. Broke that entire record up. Whether he sent me a nickel or not, I loved him, praised him, thanked him and went about my business not knowing where the next dollar was coming from. For I had spent a fortune by taking off one year and living at the same level I had lived in previous years—and spent money like water.

Then I changed that old man into the new man by changing my conversation with him. Do you know, in no time flat, unasked, a very large wonderful check came to me. No restraint. I didn't appeal at all. So I am telling you from experience that it works this way. Yet, if you are in the mood to argue, enjoy yourselves, but remember it doesn't stop there, it's going to balloon and crystallize and manifest itself in your world.

Do you know it becomes a pleasant thing after a while to carry on lovely conversations? It becomes very pleasant. Believe me, I would not deceive you; I have told you exactly what happened to me as to the promise. I have told you exactly what I have PROVEN as to the law. It will not fail you. Take the law and put it into practice NOW and know that if you carry on these conversations the promise of the 50th Psalm will take form. He will show you the salvation of God.

The salvation of God is simply, you awakened as God. That's how He shows it to you. He came and He comes into human history in the person of Jesus Christ and there is only one Jesus Christ. When it happens, you are Jesus Christ. You don't change your name. You are still Mary, Stan or John. But, when it happens, you know who you are. You walk the street still Stanley, Mary or Neville, but you know who you are.

The whole story is all about you and one day you will actually know you are the Lord Jesus Christ.

JUSTIFIED
STATES

So many people tell us we must do this, that or the other or else. Forget it. God planned everything as it has come out, and as it will be consummated. It is your Father's good pleasure to *give* you the kingdom. You do not earn it, it's not your due, it's not a reward; it's simply a gift, unmerited, and therefore you cannot lose it. The gift is irrevocable. No man can take it from you and no man can give it to you, so let no one frighten you. It is yours, and it is coming on time.

The gift is nothing less than God Himself. When He gives you the kingdom, He gives you Himself. For the kingdom is not a realm, the kingdom is a character, it's a body, and that body is perfect. Wherever you are, clothed in that body, everything around you is perfect.

Were you in the petrified forest, it would burst into foliage. If you are in the midst of broken members of society, they will all be in harmony. If you come into a world where there are blind, lame, halt, withered—instantly, as you glide by eyes that were missing come out of the nowhere and fill the empty sockets. Arms that are missing, feet missing, everything would come out of the nowhere and be made perfect because you are present. That is God's gift, which is the gift of Himself, which is His body. One day you will be clothed with that body.

"Set your hope fully upon the grace that is coming to

you at the revelation of Jesus Christ within you." That is
the unfolding within you of God and His son. This is the
hope that makes it wisdom to endure the burden of this
long, dark night of time. For as Paul said, "I consider the
sufferings of this present time not worth comparing with
the glory that is to be revealed in us."

We are told, "We are justified by His grace." Justification, in scripture, is divine acquittal. No matter what you
have ever done, you are completely acquitted.

We are told, "Those whom He foreknew He predestined to be conformed to the image of His son. Those
whom He predestined He also called. Those whom He
called He justified. Those whom He justified He also glorified." Justification is simply divine acquittal, and glorification is the gift of God Himself to you. Man matures when
he becomes his own father.

"It is the Father's good pleasure to give us the kingdom." In giving us the kingdom He gives us Himself, and in
giving us Himself, man becomes his own father. Let no one
worry you, let no one in any way suggest you must do
something to earn it. You cannot earn the kingdom. You
cannot earn this gift. It's not your due, for if it were your
due then it's not a gift. It's not given as a reward. You are
made fit for the kingdom, and your fitness is the con-
sequence and not the condition of His gift.

The minute he gives you Himself you are fitted for the
kingdom. You wear the body of God and everything in
your presence is made perfect.

The promise comes first in scripture, then we are told
He gave us a law to cushion the blows while we, as pilgrims, walk through the furnaces. We have a law, but even
the wisest of men are not aware of it.

In 1949 I was in Milwaukee and gave a series of lectures on the Bible. A man who was the head of the chemical department of Allis Chalmers attended my lectures.
One evening he said, "Neville, I can't quite go along with
you because as a chemist it is in conflict with my training.
You tell me you can go forward in time; that you can

move backwards in time; that all things *are*, and everything is *now*, this very moment. Yet you are telling me you can make things change, and it is in conflict with my training.

We have a law known as entropy. Entropy means that the past is fixed and unalterable. You cannot change it. If the past can be changed it throws everything out of kilter in my lab. I must know the past is unalterable. Like braiding a lady's hair, the braided part, that's fixed. The rest is future—Not yet braided. We are waiting to see how it will develop from the braided part because that is completely fixed and unalterable. Now you tell me it is not; that the whole vast world exists now, past, present and future. That you can go into sections of time, in a world that is finished. Well, I can't go along with that."

It's perfectly all right. I am not a chemist. I am not a scientist, so I can't argue the point. I only know my visions and I teach vision as I have experienced it. I can go into these places and the past has not passed away. I am quite sure one could go back and revise that past and change it. I know I can go forward into the future, set it up and walk across a bridge of incident to the point in time where I entered that state, and it takes on the color, the tone and the reality I assumed it to be.

In the month of November he sent me the Science News Letter dated October 15th, which contained an article about the positron, written by Richard Fineman, professor of physics at Cornell University. (Twenty years later they granted him the Nobel Prize in physics for that paper), and if I can quote it, this is it:

"The positron is a wrong way electron. It is wrong way in every sense of the word. It moves backwards in time. It moves to where it hasn't been, and speeds to where it was an instant ago. Arriving there it is bounced so hard its time sense is reversed, and it moves back to where it hasn't been."

Now that is not Neville speaking, that is Professor Fineman, and for that he got the Nobel Prize last year. He said, "It is not only backwards in that sense, but even its charge is backwards. It's a positron, it's positive and not negative, yet it is an electron."

When they first had this as theory they did not want to admit it, but it fitted in with Einstein's theory, mathematically. So they had to accept it, but no one had ever photographed it. Then someone came who photographed it in their studies of the cosmic rays. It seemed as though two were developed at a certain point, but it wasn't. The one coming back was the positron and should, if bounced, be deflected and continue on its deflected course. On the other hand it is bounced so hard it is not deflected, it's reversed and moves forward in a normal manner to where it hasn't been.

I had told him I could sit at home and go into a section of time. For instance, this is now April. I put myself in December and I see the stores all dressed for Christmas. I hear the music of Christmas, all the carols. I walk through Saks Fifth Avenue in New York City and feel all I would feel if it were true that this is the month of Christmas. Then, when I *feel* it is Christmas, I feel that things are as I desired them to be back in the month of April.

Then I open my eyes and bounce back and shock myself, because it seemed so real to me that when I came back and opened my eyes upon April I thought I was kidding myself. No, I wasn't kidding myself, for when I went forward in time quite normally, waiting out the days, the months, to the month of December, things happened as I had assumed they would when I went forward and predetermined what would happen.

Look at it this way. See the whole vast world as infinite states and you an immortal being. You enter a state and the state becomes alive. Therefore you are not to blame if you unwittingly enter a horrible state. Man, not knowing you are in a state, condemns you, but you must express the contents of the state to which you are committed.

If you enter the state of poverty you have to experience poverty. If you remain in it you must drink it to the dregs. If you go into any state and remain there you are going to drink it to the very last drop.

But you can get out of a state. You don't have to remain in it if you know it is a state. If you don't know it you identify yourself with the state and think you are it. Man has identified himself with this little body and thinks he is it. The day will come when he has to discard it because he has worn it out. As he discards it all of his friends think he died. He didn't die, for he can't die. He is an immortal being who wore a garment of flesh and blood. That same being goes into a state and, remaining in it, he resurrects it, for "I AM the resurrection and the life" of that state.

Now you can move an individual into another state with or without his consent if you so desire. Let us take the story as told us in the Book of Acts. A man who could not stand on his own feet was begging at the temple door. Peter said, "Gold and silver have I not for thee but such as I have, give I unto you, rise and walk." Instantly he rose and walked.

It doesn't mean a cripple jumped up and walked away. No one is going to jump up from a crippled state and start walking. But put your friend on his own feet by representing him to yourself as you would like him to be. That's what I am talking about when I say they are all states. Take him out of one state and put him into another. You are an immortal being. You change only when you fall into a state. Others who knew you well in one state, wonder what has happened, yet the immortal being who occupied the state has not changed.

Therefore God forgives everyone. He justifies everyone because He knows they are only in states. The Lord created every state. That's what Blake meant when he said, "I do not consider the just or the wicked to be in a supreme state, but to be every one of them states of the sleep which the soul may fall into in its deadly dreams of good and evil when it left paradise following the serpent."

Man left that heavenly state of innocence and came

into a world of experience, of educative darkness to experience generation. We are generating and multiplying these garments of flesh. The drama is from innocence, through experience, to an awakened imagination. When the imagination completely awakes, that's the divine body Jesus. That's God.

We are the pilgrims moving through states. Master the art of moving from one state to another. You are not the state. You never have been and you never will be. If you are going to condemn, condemn the state, but why condemn anything, move him out of a state into another. Move yourself out of one state into another. Others may say it can't be done; leave them alone and go about your Father's business moving from state to state as you desire it.

It all starts with a hunger, a real desire on your part. All these infinite states are simply to satisfy the hungers of men. You want to be good as you understand good to be? You want to be wealthy? All these are states. Go into the state before you are qualified, go and stay there. The state has all the things necessary to externalize itself, but you are the occupant power, you have to go into the state and dwell there. As I go into it, let me remain there. If I come back from it, like the positron, I am going to be turned around . . . I am not going to be deflected and continue my journey in the same direction only deflected; I am going to be so shocked when I open my eyes and find myself back here because the state seemed so real. But that shock turns me around and I move forward as an electron, I am not a positron anymore. Then I am moved across a bridge of incident, some series of events that will lead up to the fulfillment of what the world calls reality, but it was real when I occupied it in my imagination.

We exist in these bodies. We live in our imagination. Imagination is God, that is the divine body, Jesus.

I used to sit in my living room and although I couldn't see the chair from the telephone in the hallway, I would sit at the telephone in my imagination while my body was in the living room. Then I would assume I am at the telephone. Physically I couldn't see my body. Then, suddenly I would feel myself back on the chair and what a shock. Then from the chair I would put myself on the outside of the house and assume I am looking at the building from the outside. Then suddenly I *am* on the outside and looking at it from the outside.

Do it with your own home. Do it with anything in your room; it gets you in a state of moving. You become mobile, as it were, and it's easy then to occupy any state, for they are only states.

When someone thinks themselves so important, remember it's only a state and that state, in itself, is important to them, and anyone occupying that state must do exactly what they do. If I were in the state of Hitler I would do the same thing Hitler did, because it's a state and if I fall into it knowingly or unknowingly I've got to play that part.

Do not consider the just or the wicked to be in a supreme state, but to be every one of them states of the sleep which the soul falls into when it leaves paradise following the serpent, that serpent of generation.

You can be what you want to be if you know that all of these are only states. Then, in the end you are justified, completely exonerated. You are acquitted . . . divinely acquitted. So let no one frighten you as to what you must do to earn the kingdom. You do not *earn* the kingdom; it is your Father's good pleasure to give it to you.

It is a gift that is not your due. It's not a reward for any good things you did. If you are in a state, and you think there are good things you are doing, it is only a state. I personally find it easier living in my world to be in good states. I find it easier to be kind than to be unkind. An unkind remark hurts me more than the one who received it from me, so I find it easier to be in a kind state. Eventually you will completely awake with a gift, and the gift is God Himself. There is nothing but God in this world.

Someone called and asked me about devils. She said

she went down to a Christian Science practitioner who
now feels she is haunted with devils. Well, they teach
devils. The devil does this, the devil does that. I said, "That
is getting away from the first and greatest commandment,
the confession of faith in the Hebraic world, "Hear, O
Israel, the Lord, our God, the Lord is one." The minute
you get away from that you have a devil. There is another
God, another creator, another something. If you have two
you are going to have four, eight, sixteen, thirty-two and
so on. Always come back to the fundamental state. There
is only God, and God is your own Wonderful Human
Imagination. When you say, "I am," that's God. There is
no other, and never will be another God. He is going to
unfold himself within you, and when He awakes, *you* are
God.

Then you will be clothed in that heavenly garment. I
can't describe it other than to tell you when you are in it
you are not standing on the earth. I can only describe it as
air and fire. When you glide by this sea of imperfect
humanity you do not raise one little finger to change
them. You have no compassion because they cannot remain as they are. As you glide by, everyone is made perfect, not one is left out. It doesn't matter what he did to
lose his eyes, his arms, his legs, his tongue; in your presence he cannot remain imperfect. That is the kingdom.

It is your Father's good pleasure to give you the kingdom. So set your heart fully upon this gift, and then you
can endure the temporary ills of the world. Because we are
moving through all these things and not every moment of
time are we alert to these states. We can fall into one by
reading the newspaper or hearing a news bulletin. Fall into
it by a little conversation with a friend. We slip innocently
into a state, but the state isn't concerned. But you animate
it and make it alive when you enter it. You are the resur-
recting, living power of the world, and that power is your
own wonderful human imagination.

Put your mind at peace and don't think for one
moment by being good, as the world calls good, by attend-

ing certain services, doing and observing certain things that there is someone on the outside watching you and making the ledger in your favor; no, you are simply waiting for that appointed moment when He unveils himself. So set your hope fully on the grace that is coming to you at the revelation of Jesus Christ within you, which is the Lord and His Christ, and Christ is the son of God.

"No one can say Jesus is Lord except by the Holy Spirit," and the Holy Spirit is the remembrancer. He doesn't bring about that remembrance until the son appears, but when the son appears memory returns, and then you know who the Lord is. You wear this little garment a few more years, take it off and you are not in this world any more. You are in an entirely different world where everything is perfect because you are perfect. When you want to make yourself seen by another, *you* make that choice. They do not come in search of you and see you.

You do not see one who has already been born from above until he chooses to show himself. You do not go looking for him, because, unless you are born from above you cannot enter the kingdom, and one to whom he has already given the kingdom is not in the world, though for a little while he is telling the story from experience and not from theory.

I am telling you exactly what has happened to me. It is going to happen to every one of you. Let no one in any way try to convince you you must be a little better than you are to get the kingdom. The kingdom is your gift.

Listen to the words in the 11th chapter of Romans; "The gift and the call of God are irrevocable." No one can revoke it. Your inheritance is not only God, you are told in the 4th chapter of Romans, "You inherit the world." You don't inherit some little portion of the world, you inherit God and God owns the world; therefore, the world is your inheritance.

In the 16th Psalm, David is made to say, "The portion of my inheritance is the Lord." The son inherits the

Father. So, a man matures when he becomes his own
father. This is the great mystery of scripture. You will
inherit the Father. It is His will, and no one can break His
will. "It is your Father's good pleasure to give you the
kingdom."

When you hear people bragging how this one is better
than the other, forget it; they are judging states. That man
is richer because he is in a state richer than another state,
but the occupant of the rich state does not differ from the
occupant of the poor. The occupant of the state who is in
jail tonight does not differ from the occupant of the state
who sentenced him. One is not better than the other, for
in the eyes of God *all* are acquitted. That's justification.

"We are justified by His grace," we are told. All are
justified by His grace and grace is an unearned, unmerited
gift of God. That grace is God's last, His final gift which is
love in action, and God is love. It's the gift of Himself. He
gives you Himself, and the whole vast world is yours. So
we inherit the earth.

I hope you will start practicing. It costs you nothing to
try it and it works wonders. Put yourself in a state of
affluence, what's wrong with that? But you must move *out*
of one state in order to move *into* another. One time in my
life a twelve dollar suit was all I could afford and all I
thought I could ever afford. I got out of that state and
thought differently and now pay $250 for a suit easier
than when I had to get up twelve dollars for a suit that, if it
rained, I had to start running or I couldn't get out of it.

That is life. I simply moved from one state into another, and I learned what I couldn't do in one state I
found so easy to do in another state. . . .

For the longest time I was in a state when I couldn't
eat meat, fish, fowl, drink alcohol, smoke, sex; well, I did
nothing, but nothing. Then overnight my friend Abdullah
told me, "You are going to come back from Barbados and
you will have died." I said, "I will die?" He answered, "I
didn't say you are going to die, but you will have died. All

the things you haven't done in seven years you will be doing before you get back."

Do you know he was right? And I couldn't tell you how it happened. It just happened. In Barbados I lived in my mother's home for three months and still lived as I did in New York City. Then on my trip north, in ten days I did everything I hadn't done in seven years and I cannot tell you how it happened. I moved out of one state into another and it came as normal and as natural as it could be.

I tell you they are only states, all states of consciousness. If you can realize that, you can forgive every being in this world no matter what he is, what he plans to be or what he has done. Because in the end he is going to be justified. He is justified by the grace of God. Everyone is justified by the grace of God. He is divinely acquitted. When God acquits him, who is going to judge him? Then after justification comes glorification.

He begins with, "Those whom He foreknew . . ." He foreknew us, for "He chose us in Him before the foundation of the world." If He chose me in Him before the foundation of the world, then He knew me. And "those whom He foreknew He predestined." He predestined them to conform to the image of His son, which reflects and radiates His glory and bears the express image of Himself.

Those whom He predestined He called. "Call my sons from afar and my daughters from the end of the earth." He is calling us one by one by one, for we are so unique He can't call us in pairs. ". . . those whom He called, He also justified. Those whom He justified, He also glorified." You are destined to be glorified with God, as God.

From the pulpits of the world every Sunday morning they try to scare the people to death. They set themselves up as a criteria as to what people ought to be. In other words, "Look at me," they say, and "Follow me."

I saw a picture in the paper the other day of the son of a very prominent evangelist across the country. The son confessed he had sinned against his wife, his children and against God. I went on to read that this man takes in thirty million in tithes a year. He tells the people how they are serving God when they send him money. The father is eighty years old but still in control of thirty million a year, tax free. I wonder what he talks about. When you go into that sort of money that is big business, and you have no room in your mind's eye for any spirituality, none whatsoever. You can take that greatest of all books and make a mess of it, interpreting it as something taking place here in this secular world, and it isn't so at all.

This story is all spirituality. It's God's plan of redemption and it hasn't a thing to do with the secular world. They are telling you the future of America, of Russia, of China. No, that's not in scripture.

Take those words of our founding fathers to heart and burn them in your mind. "Our founding fathers did not believe in the future, they believed it in." They knew what they wanted as an ideal form of government and they believed it in. The last time our President Hoover spoke for the GOP was in San Francisco. He was an old man, and being an honored, wonderful man, he had the key address. He said, "Our governments, with their many forms of governments, their revolutions and their wars, in fact the rise and fall of nations could be written in terms of the rise and fall of ideas implanted in the minds of men."

Governments are not something that is forecast upon the world; you and I by our change of states make the government. Want to change the government? Change yourself.

I can tell you how to test it. Put yourself in a state you desire. Remain in that state until you wear it naturally as you would a suit of clothes. You may go in a store and buy a new suit, walk down 5th Avenue and, although no one knows you, you feel as though everyone is looking at your new suit. But after a week or two you are not self-conscious anymore. The same thing is true with a new state. Put on a new state and you feel self-conscious and think everyone knows. They don't know. Wear that state until it becomes natural. The moment it becomes natural it is going to bear the fruit of that state. "The entire space-time history of the world is laid out, and we only become aware of increasing portions of it successively."

DUALITY
OF MAN

We have only to enlarge our concept of causality to excuse everything and forgive all.

Let us turn to the 25th chapter of Genesis. "In your limbs lie nations twain, rival races from their birth. One the mastery will gain, the younger over the elder reign."

The first one is the sense man. I am now looking at this room and all within it. That is the sense man. My normal apprehension of corporeal objects (just like this room and the contents) I call sense perceived. That which is not present yet I perceive, I call *imagination*. That is destined to rule. That is the second man, the Lord from heaven.

The first man is of the earth, a man of dust. The second is from heaven. This world is a world where the dual state within every child born of woman exists. We have the physical man, the man of dust; then we have the spiritual man, the man of imagination, that is the immortal man.

When I see this picture of the duality of man and how all things are created by this hidden man, I forgive everything the physical man does. For the physical man is only a state. One being is playing all the parts. The part played by the thief is the same being playing the part of the judge who judges the thief. The murderer and the murdered are parts, but the being within is one.

Let me explain it by a simple story. Years ago when I lived in New York, two of my brothers, Victor and Lawrence, came to spend two weeks with me. They wanted to see everything they could during their visit, so I bought them fourteen shows. There was one special show my brother Lawrence wanted to see, but the papers said it was sold out. Before I left my hotel room, I simply assumed that I gave them the tickets. When we arrived at the Metropolitan, billboards advertising the show had large signs saying, "Sold Out," "No Seats Available." I got into the first line of three. It was a very long line. Then I noticed the third line from me moving more rapidly than the first and the second, so I moved over to that line.

As I approached the window, a tall blonde man, about 6'4", stretched his hand up over my head and diverted the ticket teller's attention as he asked a question, while the one in front of me was buying seats for some other opera. He leaves and by now the tall blonde man is at the door when the ticket salesman said, "He only gave me three dollars." I turned around and screamed at the tall blonde, "Sir." He looked around and I said, "Come back here. You are wanted." He came back like a little child. After some discussion, the man took out the money and paid for the tickets. Then I said to the teller, "I want two tickets for tonight's show in the horseshoe circle, center." He said, "Yes, sir." Then he took the tickets from what is called the VIP reserve (they always keep a few out for those coming called the very important people.) Well, I certainly am not a very important person, but I saved him from the loss of twenty dollars.

Now, a state called a thief. These two men had chosen to be thieves in their world. They are con men. It's perfectly all right. "God made everything for its purpose, even the wicked for the time of trouble." Read that in the 16th chapter, the 4th verse of Proverbs. "He made everything for its purpose, even the wicked for the day of trouble."

The day of trouble may not be a war. I was troubled as to how to get these tickets. That's a moment of trouble. I

simply assumed I had them and I played my part in my
imagination before I left my hotel room. Then two who
have already given themselves over to the state of a thief
had to come into the line. I took the first line, then moved
to the third. So they come to the third line and play their
part beautifully.

If they had not done what they did, I would not have
received those tickets, because I am not a VIP. They find it
easier being con men. There are those who are pickpockets. All right, that's their part and they play it. Now
you play your part beautifully and one of them could be
instrumental in giving you what you want in this world.
They played their part, should I not forgive them?

There are infinite states in this world. All you have to
do is forgive states. Play your part and every state necessary to make your part come to fulfillment will be present
at the moment you need it.

"In your limbs lie nations twain, rival races from their
birth. One the mastery shall gain. The younger over the
elder reign." The younger is the second and the second
man is the man from heaven. That man is your own wonderful human imagination, who is God. There is no other
God. That is the Lord from heaven. The outer man that
clothes him is under compulsion to fulfill the commands
of the inner man. Everyone is falling into states, infinite
states.

To understand this world, you must think in terms of
states. "He has made everything for its purpose, even the
wicked for the day of trouble." You don't have to think of
which one will do it; forget who will play the part. I never
saw that man or his partner in their little crime before.
That was their choice in life. There are those who have
chosen to be pickpockets for the rest of their lives. If they
are caught in the act, that's part of the game. They have
chosen that part to play.

There are those who have chosen parts to play like Mr.
Hoover who just departed this world. Others chose other

parts. Either wisely or unwisely we fall into these states, but when the inner man begins to awake, he selects his part wisely. It's entirely up to us.

Everything in this world you want to be, you can be if you know they are only states. Move into the state. The occupant of any state does not differ from the occupant of any other state. The one who played the part that day of the con man is God. God is playing all the parts. All we have to do is expand our concept of causality to excuse everything and forgive everyone in this world. I forgave him because he was instrumental in getting me the two seats I desired. Were he not playing that part at that moment, I would not have had my tickets.

But, before I left the hotel room, I simply assumed my brothers had their seats for the show and came home thrilled beyond measure. We went down and seemingly no hope. I wasn't concerned about any hope. What caused me to move to the third window? The Father in me. He knew which one is going to play what part, because they are all in states and my deeper self is fully aware of all the states in the world. If you can play a part to aid me in the fulfillment of my dream, you will play it. If I need a thief, there must be a thief somewhere. He was a thief and he played a far better part for my getting the tickets than if he were an honest man. If he came up and played the part of an honest man, then the man would have said to me, "We have no tickets, don't you see the signs?" But a thief made it possible for me to get my tickets.

When you understand this, you forgive every being in the world. They are all playing their parts. Don't condemn anyone, because everyone will be instrumental in fulfilling your dream if you know this law. It's all infinite states. But remember, you are awakening to the reality of the second man.

In this room, my simple apprehension of corporeal objects, the things on the wall, the chairs, all this to my sense man is reality. Then I think of something entirely different that is called only imagination, and that is the second man. What do I want in place of what my senses are telling me? Let me now enter into that state, live in it as though it were true, and I will move forward in that state.

An idea that is only an idea produces nothing and does nothing. It must be *felt,* actually felt, so it awakens within oneself certain sensations, certain motor actions in order to be effective. What would the feeling be like if it were true? Dwell upon that until the feeling awakes within you these sensations. For imagination is spiritual sensation. That is the creative being in you.

It's not just to entertain an idea. The idea must produce in you this feeling which is a sensation, but it must be a feeling. What would the feeling be like if it were true? You dwell upon it until you catch the feeling. As Churchill said, "The mood determines the fortunes of people rather than the fortunes the mood." The mood *precedes* the fortunes.

What would you want in this world? Contemplate it. What would the feeling be like if you had it? What would it be like if it were true? That is the story of scripture. If I could only feel I am already the man I want to be. That I am already the woman I want to be, then it is not only an idea which, as an idea without feeling will produce nothing, now it has everything. Because in the story he said to the second man, "Come close, my son, that I may feel you." The secret is in the feeling. Esau went out. He is the first man covered with hair, the outer man, and Jacob is the inner man, the man of imagination who is hairless. It isn't two little boys, these are only symbols. It's all in man. "Come close, my son, that I may feel you." The father feels him and he feels externally real. You, too, can do it.

There is no flower in your hand, but you can feel the soft velvet feeling of a rose. You can smell a rose though it's not physically present. Try it. Try all these things with the inner man. When you actually feel it, you raise your imagination to the point of sensation, to vision, then the

whole thing is done. In a way you do not know, it is going
to happen even if it takes a thief to aid you. Then you
forgive the thief.

All we have to do is widen, a little bit, our concept of
casuality to forgive all in the world, to excuse everything
in the world, for they are playing their parts. Tonight if
you want a bigger job, more money, you name it. There
may be a thief who is going to aid you in the getting and
he will do it without knowing he is doing it. Don't judge
him, don't condemn him; simply go forward knowing, "I
have ways and means the physical man knows not of. My
ways (the inner man's ways) are past finding out." Simply
go forward in the assumption you have already achieved
what now is only a wish as far as the world is concerned,
but enter into the wish as though it is already fulfilled.

What would the feeling be like? "Come near, my son,
that I may *feel* you. Your voice is the voice of Jacob, but
your hands, your neck and your scent, you have the *feel* of
my son Esau." (Esau is the outer world.) He gives empha-
sis to feeling; it transcends the voice. The voice was Jacob,
but the feeling, the touch was that of an external world.
He could feel the external world. It was a self deception.
He deceived himself into believing that what he desired, he
had. It's not two little boys born of a woman. All this is
parable. The whole story of the Bible is all parabolic.

Do you know what you want? Really what you want?
If you do, do the same thing I did in getting the two seats.
Do what I did when I was locked out completely from
marrying the girl I wanted to marry. I simply assumed she
slept there and I slept here. Then in one week my wife did
an act which certainly I must forgive. To the eyes of the
world she was condemned for taking what she did not pay
for, yet because of that act, I got my freedom. Then who
is the culprit? Am I not? If there is any culprit in this
world, it is God. There is nothing but God. God is doing all
in this world. He created everything in this world. If, in
me, He is the second man and the second man is my imagination and that is God, then man is all imagination, and

God is man and exists in us and we in him. The eternal body of man is the imagination and that is God Himself.

I, in my imagination, slept as though I was happily married to a girl the laws of New York State state I could never get because of my entanglement with my first wife. Then, in one week, she performed an act which was judged harshly by society. Yet she was the instrument of my getting my freedom to marry the girl who now is the mother of my daughter. So how can I blame her who performed the act? She was in a state. Who did it? I did it. I did it by simply assuming I was free.

Learn to forgive everyone in this world. They are all playing their parts. In my own case I have seen thieves, all kinds of people play their parts. They were instruments in the fulfillment of my desires, so how can I ever condemn them?

The last cry on the cross is, "Father forgive them, they know not what they do." Forgive them, for the whole vast world is playing their part automatically, unwittingly, for one who is awake and knows exactly what he is doing. For God in everyone is the same God. There aren't two gods, there is only One. That God is your own Wonderful Human Imagination. When you say, "I am," that's God.

Boldly claim you are the man, the woman you want to be, and walk in that assumption as though it were true; then let all these sleeping states play their part. May I tell you, in spite of what they appear to be, they are sound, sound asleep. They do not know what they are doing. But don't condemn. If there is any condemnation of the part, where is the author? Send for the author, for he wrote the part. If there is any praise or any condemnation, give it to the author.

In this wonderful world of ours, we are infinite states and everyone is in a state. But the one being in one state is the one being in all states. There is only one player. God only acts and is in existing beings or men. He is in all the states and His name in all states is I AM.

Someone may chose the part of a thief. He thinks it's

easier than getting up and going to work; all right, he has chosen that part if he does it deliberately, or he might have fallen into it through the habit of others and then it is unwittingly. But he will also pay the price. That is the one thing he has to consider. He will pay the price because the part has a price with it. But in spite of that he can be used in the fulfillment of your dream.

Many of you have had dreams of death recently. May I tell you it's a healthy, healthy sign. Dreams are egocentric. You cannot grow and not outgrow in this world. To outgrow is to die. You die to one state and move into another state. Anyone dreaming of death, be thankful, for as Paul said, "I die daily." Every day he grows. If he did not die, everyday, then he didn't grow that day. So death is a beautiful symbol of your growth. You are growing, that's why you see yourself buried or in a tomb. It's simply an expansion of consciousness. You die to one state as you enter a greater state of consciousness. Death has nothing to do with the physical body, because you don't die anyway, not really; nothing dies. It's always an expansion and expansion and expansion. So when you do see yourself being buried, give thanks, for you have died to your former beliefs. New ideas have called you to an expansion of yourself, so the old man dies that the new man may live.

A seed must fall into the ground and die before it can be made alive. If it does not fall into the ground and die, it cannot bring forth fruit. It simply remains what it is, was before. If it dies, it bears much fruit. So don't be afraid of any vision of death. Death is the most glorious symbol in the mysteries of the expansion of consciousness. Man is expanding and expanding and expanding in this world. Then one day his wonderful imagination will awaken and that is God. Then he sees the whole vast world as sleepers. All sleepers and how can you condemn the sleeper? He played his part and played it beautifully.

I can see all these things in my world where people played so many marvelous parts. They were sound asleep and they thought they were so alert and going to get the better of me. Their attempt was exactly what I needed to move on. I forgive all the thieves that came into my world. Even those who actually took from my pocket by not giving me what the contract called for. I thanked them because it allowed me to become all the more secure on my own feet and not think for one second I depended upon them or upon anyone else in this world. Let them go their way. They are all sound, sound asleep playing their parts.

"In your limbs lie nations twain, rival races from their birth. One the mastery will gain, the younger over the elder reign." See that that younger one actually reigns. The younger one is your imagination. The older one is your sense man. These are the facts of life. What is my bank account? Do I owe more than the bank account has in it now? That is Esau's judgment. Now Jacob puts in fifty times what is there now. In my mind's eye, I have deposited fifty times more than is there. How it is going to happen, I don't know. But it will happen, for God plays all the parts in the world. There is nothing but God. You say, "I AM." That's God. That is the Lord Jesus within you. That is your immortal being that cannot die. That is your eternal self.

Imagination is not some vague essence. It is a body, a reality, an infinite body that is so perfect when it is awakened that in its presence everything is made perfect. But while it is awakening, it exercises that power and draws into its world everyone that can play the part for the fulfillment of its dream.

I have tried to make it as clear as I can. I hope you will go forward knowing who you are. You are a dual being, but the first man is of the dust and to dust he returns. That is the man of earth. The second man is the Lord from heaven and he cannot die. That's your own wonderful human imagination. But it sleeps embodied in this tomb (this body of dust you wear is God's tomb). One day it will awaken and the symbolism of scripture will surround you. It is perfect. It is true. Everything told in scripture as to his birth you are going to experience, and when your imagination awakens you trust no one but it. Only this being within you do you really worship. You will know who you are when you begin to feel there is something alive within you, and it's your *own* wonderful human imagination.

You go to bed at night, and, while the body sleeps, you are awake teaching, instructing and doing so many marvelous things. Trying to awaken everyone who is called to you.

We are all given a certain number. They are drawn to you and you must awaken them. In the end you will go back and be able to say, "I have accomplished the work thou gavest me to do. Now glorify me with thine own self, with the glory that I had with thee before that the world was."

I gave that up to come down and assume the limitation of being in a garment of flesh and blood. Now I have finished the work. "Return unto me the glory that is mine. The glory that I had with thee before that the world was." Then you take off this garment and return to your glory having told it as best you could.

May you all have dreams of dying, meaning that you are outgrowing a certain state. For, you cannot grow and not outgrow. No one can grow and not outgrow. If I bought a pair of new shoes today for a child and within a week they are buckling, for his foot has grown, and I insist that because they are new he must wear them, I am going to cripple that child. Take them off regardless of what I paid for them and get shoes that fit now. He is growing and growing; he will outgrow.

So don't try to hold the mind into a little frame that was given you at birth. When you were born into this world, you were told that Jesus is this and God is this and your church is the only place where you can ever be saved. You go to church every Sunday and follow all these rituals; then like a shoe on your foot, one day you can't stand it; it is painful and you've got to take off that shoe and outgrow it.

May I repeat, "In your limbs are nations twain," one is the sense man who sees and accepts as fact what reason dictates and what the senses dictate. No one sees the other, but he is not a vapor, he is not some peculiar essence. He is an actual being, an immortal body, but it's asleep. It's asleep in you, but it's creative. That's the creative one in you and that one will one day awaken, and when he awakens he is God Himself.

GATHERED
ONE
BY ONE

We are told in Isaiah, "You shall be gathered one by one, O people of Israel." An Israelite is not a descendant of Abraham after the flesh, but the called, the chosen, the elect of any race or nation. God calls individuals to enter His body before they are members of it, and we are called one by one when we are on the outside as descendants of Adam. Adam must still reproduce himself in those who are born his children. Only by an intervention of some new nature could there be an exhaltation of the old.

Our last world war certainly proved that. Take a wonderful, marvelous nation, a hundred million intelligent people, possibly the highest standard in the world educationally speaking. We have their history of music, their history of science, and overnight they are turned into a madhouse, proving that Cain is still within the heart of everyone that he could slaughter his brother.

Man has tried over and over again to bring about a social regeneration in mankind and he has always failed. You cannot do it until the new nature is grafted onto this old. God calls individuals to enter His body and He calls us one by one.

Let me share with you my experience back in 1929. I did not know how literally true the Bible was until it began to unfold itself within me. I was a dancer, living in a

hotel. Early in the morning, maybe about three-thirty or
four o'clock, I was taken in spirit into the Divine Council
where the gods hold converse. There I saw an angelic being
at an open ledger. She turned and looked into my face;
then, taking a quill pen, she made a note in the open book.

From there I was taken into the presence of Infinite
Love, the Ancient of Days just as described in the 7th
chapter of the Book of Daniel. He looked at me and asked,
"What is the greatest thing in the world?" I answered in
the words of Paul, "Faith, hope and love, but the greatest
of these is love." With that he embraced me, our bodies
fused and we became one body.

Paul tells us, "He who is united to the Lord becomes
one spirit with Him. One body, one Spirit, one hope, one
Lord, one faith, one baptism, one God and Father of them
all, who is above all, through all and in all." In that union I
felt infinite love without loss of my identity. I was still
individualized, but I have never known such intensity of
love; God truly is love.

Thirty years later, in the summer of '59, that union,
that graft began to bear fruit. It took thirty years for the
graft to take. Then the gift of God began to move down-
ward from that which was collective to me the individual.
For He said, "Let US . . ." (that is a collective being) ". . .
make man in our image." Then the heavenly gifts come
down from that which was collective to that which is
individual.

You can analyze the gifts. Infinite power. No man on
earth knows this power until he has tasted of it. I have
come upon a scene just like this and realized it was not
independent of my perception of it. The whole thing was
animated from within me. Prior to that moment I thought
everything was completely independent of my perception
of it, and then I realized it was not so at all. I knew the
whole vast world was (and is) myself pushed out. To
prove it I stopped the activity within myself, and as I did
everything froze . . . but everything.

The waiter walking, walked not. The diners dining,

dined not. The leaves falling, fell not. The bird in flight, flew not and everything was perfectly still. I examined it and it was all dead as though made of clay. The animating power that made it appear to be alive was all within me. That is the power I speak of. That is the power in store for everyone after he is called and incorporated into the body of God. Wisdom will come, unlike anything known to man. You will have an innate knowledge of all things without any so-called scholastic background.

I can't tell you the thrill I felt after being incorporated into His body that night. Then I stood before Infinite Might (another aspect of God). He didn't use His lips, yet I heard the words He thought, "Time to act." Then a voice from the sky said "Down with the bluebloods;" then Infinite Power said to me, "Time to act."

Then I was whirled out of that wonderful group to find myself once more encased in this little garment of flesh, this garment of Adam with all of its weaknesses, all of its limitations, and I certainly had many. That incubation, that pregnancy, as it were, ran from July 1929 to July 1959.

Thirty years later, without warning, the drama began to unfold within me. Then I knew what it really was to be born of God. Born not of blood, nor of the will of the flesh, nor of the will of man, but of God. Born out of my own skull, for that is where you are born.

But you are born out of the skull of God, for that's where you are. That's where everyone is. It's like unnumbered brain cells in the mind of a divine dreamer and every cell is precious to him. The cell, reflected in this world of Adam is an individual, male or female. Every cell *must* awaken within that divine brain. God is dreaming the dream of life. He is dreaming you. He is dreaming He is I. In my case He awoke in 1959 and all the symbolism of scripture unfolded itself before my vision.

I can tell you from my own experience, you are in for the most marvelous treat in the world when God's purpose unfolds itself within you, as an individual. You are too

precious to be called even with one more. They can't call
you collectively; that's not good enough. You are individualized in God and He calls you as an individual before
you are born, before you are a member of His body. Then
you are grafted through that union with God. Only
through such fusion (which is a graft upon this body of
Adam) could there be a transcending or exhaltation of the
old man, the old nature.

We have the Humanist society: cultured, wonderful,
intelligent men and women who believe they can change
society by living a certain life. That's what Germany
thought. They thought they could change the horrors of
the old regime in Russia, but they got one worse than any
Czar in the world, one who could slaughter twenty million
with impunity. Hitler could slaughter millions with impunity and he was insane by any standard in the world.

I say to everyone, you can try from now until the end
of time, but the change will only take place by the grafting
of a completely new nature, and it is a gift. We are told in
scripture, "The law was given by Moses, but grace and
truth came through Jesus Christ."

Who is Jesus Christ? Read the last chapter of Revelations, "Go unto the churches and say this, I am the root
and the offspring of David, the bright morning star." I am
both the root and the offspring. He identifies the root with
the offspring and leaves David in the middle.

Who is David? David is the symbol of humanity. If you
took all the generations of men and all of their experiences, fused them into one grand whole, that concentrated
time to which they are all gathered and now personified
will come out as the eternal youth David. All the generations and all of their experiences, if personified, will invariably come out as the eternal youth of scripture named
David. That's the son of God.

Jesus is another name for Jehovah, the Lord, that's his
son. Then who is his grandson? He said, "I am the root and
the offspring of David." He identifies the grandson and the
grandfather as the same being. God is begetting Himself.

Out of humanity He is drawing forth that which is buried
in man. What is buried in man? God. By that fashion you
are bearing God. Then, in the fullness of time He brings
Himself forward. "I will gather you one by one, O people
of Israel."

Israel is the state of the called, the chosen, the elect. It
hasn't a thing to do with any physical descent. You cannot
transform Adam by any attempt made by the rational
mind. You can only transform and exhalt that being by a
new nature which is a gift; it is grace. "Grace and truth
came through Jesus Christ."

Jesus Christ is not some little being who lived two
thousand years ago, as taught by our priesthoods of the
world. Jesus Christ is *in* you right now. Jesus is your own
wonderful human imagination. That is the Lord.

When you say, "I am," that's God. He has no other
name. He is buried in you awaiting the call. When you are
called you actually stand in the presence of the Risen
Lord, the Ancient of Days. He will ask you, undoubtedly,
the same question He asked of me, and you will answer
promptly as though divinely prompted.

I had no idea I would be taken there or what I would
be asked, yet is seemed the most natural thing that could
happen to me. I stood in the presence of the recording
angel and my name was checked off as told us in the Book
of Daniel, the 12th chapter, "If your name be in the book
of life." When those came back and bragged about the
things they did in the name of Jesus, he said, "It is far
better that your name be written in the book of life than
that you did these things."

What are these things but simply things that excite the
mind of man. To cure this one, to give this one wealth,
that one health? No. I can assure you your name is written
there because you are carrying the name of God.

Before you say your name you must first say, "I am."
That's His name. So your name is in the book. The day
will come He will call you. You will be called when you
least expect it. Your name will be checked off, and you

will stand in the presence of the Ancient of Days, and you have never seen such love in your life. Infinite love. When He embraces you, you *feel* what love really is.

No one can describe it in mortal words. If I were the greatest poet in the world I could not describe that feeling, that love. It's sheer ecstasy. Then to be sent out with the words, "Down with the bluebloods." It hasn't a thing to do with the so-called social world, no; leave them alone just as they are. If they feel themselves important and want to feel they are the jet set, encourage them; that hasn't a thing to do with it. It means "church protocol, all external services, anything that leads the mind outside of self." Down with it. It does no good whatsoever to the awakening of the being within you.

These are the words that came out of the heavens when He who was Infintie Power said to me, "Time to Act." Now God only acts, and is, in existing beings or men. How does He act? He acts in your imagination. When you imagine a state, that's God in action. Can you believe in the reality of that imaginal state? If you can, that imaginal state will externalize itself and become a fact within your world. If you cannot believe in the reality of the state imagined, then you do not trust God. You are still looking for a God on the outside of self and you will look in vain, for God is within you. Your own Wonderful Human Imagination is God.

If I use the word God, or Jesus, or Lord, and it conveys to you the sense of an existant something outside of you, you have a false Lord, a false Jesus, a false God, for He is within you. You are told, "Do you not realize Jesus Christ is in you? Unless, of course, you fail to meet the test." Then comes the challenge, "Test yourself and see."

You have just received the test. Did you have the idea of some Jesus on the outside? Then you failed the test. When I said God, did your mind jump on the outside to some being other than self? Then you failed the test. He is within you forever and forever. This is the Lord of whom I speak.

All things are possible to God, and if I have found Him within me and He only acts and is in existing beings or men, I must find out how He acts. He acts by an imaginal act. Now all that I am called upon to do in this world is to believe in my imaginal act. His ways are higher than my ways, as told us in the 55th chapter of Isaiah, and His thoughts higher than the thoughts of men. So I must leave it entirely up to that imaginal act to find the means to externalize itself. It will if I am faithful.

We speak of Adam as the physical man, the outer man, but do not look upon Abraham as a physical man. Look upon Abraham as the being of faith who could believe all things possible to the God he discovered. He went into a land that was not his to be a sojourner there and all of his descendants for four hundred years, confident that God could do what he said he would, and it was accounted unto him for righteousness.

What is righteousness? Righteousness is the name given in scripture to the individual who fulfills the conditions imposed upon him. After Paul had fought the good fight and finished the race, he said there was laid up for him the Crown of Righteousness, for he had kept the faith. After he saw the vision he did not waver from it.

What is the Crown of Righteousness? The unveiling *in* man of Jesus Christ. He unveils the Christ and the Christ is David. That is the Son of God. Humanity personified as a single, eternal youth is David.

Jesus is the Lord and he unveils the son and the son reveals the Lord as you. You cannot bring forth other than the root. "If the root be holy," as we are told, "so are the branches. You must be holy, for I, the Lord your God, am holy."

You must be holy, for if you are ingrafted into that which is holy, then when you come out you have to bear the fruit of holiness. You can't bear other than what the root is.

Holiness does not mean what the world teaches, it means wholeness, it means perfection. You cannot take from or add to that which is perfect. If you take from the smallest little thing from the perfect picture it ceases to be perfect. If you add to it, then it is no longer perfect; therefore you cannot take from or add to that which is perfect. So, "Be ye perfect as your father in heaven is perfect;" be whole, be complete.

We are told, "He who began a good work *in* you will bring it to completion." When? "At the day of Jesus Christ." When He unveils His son within you. At the very moment he unveils His son in you, He unveils you as God the Father, for it takes the son to reveal the Father and only the Father knows the son. The minute you see the son you know who you are. When the work is complete and made perfect, He unveils Jesus Christ, for you will see the son and the son will tell you who you are.

In the 4th chapter of Ephesians he speaks of a knowledge, a strange knowledge of the Son of God. He doesn't name him, he doesn't call him Christ, Jesus or David. "He will bring you to the knowledge of the Son of God." When you come to that knowledge, it is because you see Him and when you see Him you know who you are. Then you know who the Christ is. Then you know who the Son of God is.

Humanity is His son. Not one member can be lost, but out of each will come God Himself. But you can only bring forth that Son of God by grafting God onto this tree that is human. The tree of Adam, because you can do anything with Adam and you cannot change him, for all things must bring forth after their kind. That law of identical harvest was established in the very first chapter of Genesis and confirmed in the very last part of the 8th chapter. All things bring forth after their kind and you can't change it.

Adam brought forth Cain who murdered his brother. In everyone there is that Cain as nations and society have proved. You can have all the sweet, lovely thoughts in the world concerning regenerating society, but you aren't going to do it. Overnight those who think themselves so above it all will find one member of the family go berserk. Not insane, but he or she acts as though insane by their behavior, and you never thought for one moment it could ever happen to them, for they were always so prominent, so altogether right in everything they did, but it happens because it is part of the nature of Adam. Adam must still bring forth his own likeness in those who are born his children. He has to bring forth himself. That's what we call "nature" in this world.

That principle upon which we depend for sameness of form in transmitted life. Do you know what kind of tree that is? Wait until the season of its bearing and you will know from the fruit it bears the nature of the tree. If you take the fruit and plant it, it is going to bear exactly what the tree bore. It cannot change. It's going to simply continue to reproduce its kind.

When God grafts Himself to man, man is baptized. We have a baptismal rite in this world, I know my mother baptized me when I was about three or four weeks old. We were all baptized, and she really believed that that little act was in some strange way a momentous thing in my life. As a Christain she was taught that something happened. No, nothing happened except I may have possibly jumped in the cold water, but it certainly didn't do anything to me. There are those who are completely immersed and believe something is going to happen. I have watched them and years later they are just as violent as they were before they jumped into the water, for not a thing had happened to them.

No, baptism is when God embraces you. How could He take billions of us and embrace us? Don't ask me how but He will. "I will gather you one by one, O people of Israel." Read it in the 27th chapter of the Book of Isaiah. We are gathered one by one; not two by two but one by one; that's how precious you are.

If I must be holy it is because the Lord God is holy. I cannot be holy by any effort of my own, but only if He

grafts Himself upon me, and He does. That was His purpose in the beginning. When we, the sons of God, came
down into humanity and caused man to breathe, we did
not have any contact with the heavenly world we left. We
did not have to pretend; we had to actually assume the
restrictions and the limitations of man.

If I came here, knowing I am the son of God, then I
could not play the part of man. We are told in the 11th
chapter of the Book of Romans: "He has consigned all
men to disobedience that He may have mercy upon all." In
order for you to understand the mercy of God, all men
have been consigned to disobedience. But the gifts and the
promise of God are irrevocable, so don't dispair.

We have the gift on the outside in the form of written
chronicles, the Bible. That's God's gift to us. Then He gives
us the internal word that will one day awake within us and
enlighten that book. The whole book will become alive
when the word, which is the engrafted word, unfolds within us.

When He embraces you, that is the graft, and you
receive the Word. Then you see the relationship between
the written word and the living word which is subjectively
received. One is objectively given and the other subjectively given. Then in good time it unfolds within you and
you know the truth of scripture.

When Paul speaks of the unity of the faith, he means
that the Old Testament and the New Testament are really
one faith, and he is asking all to see the unity of that faith.
Here is the tree of Israel and here is its fruit to prove the
nature of that tree. That tree will be grafted and the living
word will come out to interpret the written word.

Disraeli was right when he said, "Christianity is only
the fulfillment of Judaism." If it was not a great Jew who
said that, you might question it, but here is a brilliant, brilliant mind, the great Benjamin Disraeli. He never denied he
was a Jew. His very name is Israel. Disraeli is "of Israel."
He never denied that he was Benjamin of the tribe of
Benjamin. When England was at its very peak of power he

was the Prime Minister, yet Paul, preceding him by two thousand years, called upon us all to see the unity of the faith and asks us to keep it and stop being children, being torn by the winds of doctrines.

If you can see it you will fall heir to the wisdom of God, which will put to not all the wisdom of man. You will find yourself receiving the power that is God. The whole vast world is yourself pushed out and its reality is in you. It has its roots in you and you can start it and stop it at will. You can change the motivation and it will think it initiated the change. But you will not exercise this power until you are engrafted into the body. You are called and enter the body of God before you are a member of it. You are only a member after you are born from above. For no one can enter the kingdom unless he is born from above.

When you are born from above you become as God is, and all the powers of God slowly unfold within you. He didn't give you a little measure; He gave you the fullness of himself. At Calvary God literally became as we are, and at Bethlehem we literally become as God is.

The churches of the world will not tell you this story on Good Friday. They are going to see a man on a piece of wood, and that isn't so at all. This (body) is the cross God wears. This (Adam) is the cross. He is nailed on it. Vortices hold me here, but by the mercy of God and the grace of God, He engrafted Himself upon me when I answered His question correctly; then He embraced me, we fused and became one. Being united to the Lord I became one Spirit with him.

These are the seven statements in Ephesians; you will read it in the 4th chapter, "One body, one Spirit, one hope, one Lord . . ." all the way through to "one God and Father of us all." You are that God and Father when His son appears before you. You are that Father, therefore you are that God. It's the same God. There is no room for another.

Everyone is destined to awaken as God. In the meanwhile use the law. The law came through Moses, but take it

IMMORTAL MAN

as it is interpreted in the Sermon on the Mount, as a psychological law rather than a physical law.

He said, "You have heard it said of old, thou shalt not commit adultery, but I say unto you, any man who looks lustfully on a woman has already committed the act with her in his heart." That's a physhological interpretation of the law.

I may look upon a woman lustfully and not have the courage to go through with the act because I contemplate the consequences, but He tells me that's not enough. The minute you contemplated the act, you performed it in you imagination and there are those, in you, who witnessed it. Those in the divine world see all, they hear all. "Those in great eternity who contemplate on death" (this is the world of death where everything appears, it waxes, it wanes and disappears), "say this: 'What seems to be is, to those to whom it seems to be, and is productive of the most dreadful consequences to those to whom it seems to be.' Even of torment, despair and eternal death. But divine mercy steps beyond and redeems man in the body of Jesus." Even though you have done it (and we all have done it), divine mercy will redeem you. When He has engrafted Himself upon you, your whole past will be obliterated; it will mean nothing.

This is not an encouragement to go out and do all the things you wouldn't have others do to you. Just live your own wonderful, noble life; but what seems to be, is.

Can you now, at this very moment, assume the feeling of your wish fulfilled and drench that feeling to the point where you are saturated with it and believe in the reality of that act? If you can, that act is going to externalize itself. What would the feeling be like if it were true? Contemplate that feeling. Put it on as you would a suit of clothes and walk as though it is true. Remain faithful to that vision, sleep in it as though it is true and it will become true, for what seems to be is to those to whom it seems to be.

Can you sleep as though you were the woman, the man

you would like to be in spite of reason dictating you are
not, in spite of your senses telling you you are not? Can
you ignore your reason and your senses and dare to assume
you are what you want to be and sleep in that assumption?
If you do it will come to pass.

You are told, "When you pray, believe that you have
received, and you will." Can you pray in that form, for
that's the only successful prayer in the world. Begging is
not going to do it, for when you beg you are confessing
you don't have it. You've got to appropriate it. It is a
subjective appropriation of the objective hope. That's praying. I subjectively appropriate what I hope for externally.
Then, in a way I do not know, it comes into my world and
confronts me. Many of us, confronted by these things,
can't remember when we did it in imagination. But not a
thing could come in any other way.

Every natural effect has a spiritual cause and not a
natural. A natural cause only seems, it is the delusion of
the fading memory. Man doesn't remember. So when he is
confronted with his own harvest he denies it. He can't
believe for one moment that he, in some idle moment,
imagined such a thing. But it couldn't happen any other
way; it happened because he imagined it.

I tell you, you can be the man, the woman you want
to be in this world. But you are going to be that which
God has planned for you, for He is going to give you
Himself. When He gives you Himself it is going to come
suddenly and without warning. There will be a period of
incubation between the graft and its budding; in my own
case it took thirty years after the graft, so they said, "He
began his ministry when he was about thirty years of age."
It's all subjective.

A simple man, in a simple family, with at least four
brothers as they are named in the Book of Mark, and at
least two sisters, for the plural is used, "and his sisters are
with us this day." A simple being had the graft, it unfolded
within him and he told his story. Because they knew his
background they didn't believe it, for they did not see the

mystery behind what he was talking about. They thought
he was trying to balloon a little personality. No. He is
telling the mystery of God's purpose. He is telling the
mystery of the Father and the Son, for he could say, "I am
the Father, for the Father and I are one." He is the offspring and the root. He knows who David is, for David is
the sum total of humanity. When he calls you Father, then
you know who you really are.

IMAGINATION
PLUS
FAITH

Imagination plus faith are the realities out of which man fashions his world. What do I mean by imagination? I mean God. Man is all imagination, and God is man and exists in us and we in Him. The eternal body of man is the imagination and that is God Himself; the divine body Jesus, we are his members.

It's entirely up to us what we imagine, but we are told, "Without faith it is impossible to please him." Now, I can tell you that your own Wonderful Human Imagination is God, but I can't persuade you to the point of conviction. You have to become self-persuaded through experience, for imagination is the sole cause of the phenomena of life.

If you know that your own Wonderful Human Imagination is God you cannot fail in achieving your objectives. "All things are possible to him who believes." In that statement Mark equates man with God, for "With God all things are possible."

In Matthew the story is told of a rich young man who wanted to enter the kingdom of heaven. Jesus said, "Sell all you have and follow me." But the rich man was disheartened because he had so many possessions. Then Jesus said, "It is easier for a camel to pass through the eye of a needle than for a rich man to enter heaven." His disciples asked, "Who then can be saved?" He answered, "With men it is impossible, but with God all things are possible."

With men who do not know who they are, that's what
he means. With men who do now know the Lord's name.
First I must know His name, for "Those who know the
name put their trust in thee, for thou, O Lord, would not
forsake those who seek thee.

Let us look for His name as revealed in scripture.
"Moses said to God, 'If I go to the Israelites and I say to
them that the God of your forefathers has sent me to you'
and they say to me 'What is His name,' what shall I say?
Then God said to Moses, 'Say I AM that is who I AM. Say
I AM hath sent you for that is my name forever and forever, and by this name I shall be known throughout all
generations.' " I have no other name.

Just be aware. To be aware is to say "I AM." Without
uttering a sound but just being aware, that I AMness is
God. That's what I mean by imagination.

What is faith? We are told in the 11th chapter of
Hebrews that "Faith is the assurance of things hoped for,
the evidence of things not seen. By faith we understand
that the world was created by the word of God, so that
things which are seen were made out of things that do not
appear, and without faith it is impossible to please Him.
He calls a thing that is not seen as though it were and the
unseen becomes seen."

Having found that God is my own Wonderful Human
Imagination, how would I go about creating something
that seems either difficult or impossible? Naturally, I start
with God. The most blessed gift in the world is a strong,
vivid imagination, a clear idea, and a determinate vision of
things as I would like them to be.

Then, in my mind I conjure a scene which would imply
the fulfillment of my dream. See it clearly, give it all the
tones of reality, as much sensory vividness as I can, and
believe in that imaginal act. Have it so fixed in my mind
that I am oblivious to all things round about me that
would deny it, then walk in the assumption it is so.

Assume the feeling of the wish fulfilled and simply
ignore everything that denies it. Then I am calling a thing

that is not now seen as though it were seen, and that unseen state will become seen.

I tell you I know this from my own experience. It never fails, but we are the operant power. Knowing what to do is one thing, but doing it is another. Will you do it? To know it, all well and good, but will you do it? "Those who know thy name put their trust in thee."

I may be a shock to the whole vast world, but I cannot avoid telling the story. I have experienced it. I can only share with you what I know, and I am telling you that if you dare to assume the feeling of the wish fulfilled and walk in the assumption that it is so, ignoring the senses, ignoring the facts of life that deny it, in a way you do not know it will become a reality in your world. This is what I mean by imagination plus faith. These are the realities out of which we fashion our world.

I was drafted in 1942 at the age of thirty-eight. I knew I didn't want any part of it, nevertheless I was drafted and sent to Louisiana. After three months in boot training I decided I would do something about it by applying this principle. First of all I asked for an honorary discharge. A regulation had come down from Washington that if a man was thirty-eight before March 1, 1943, he was eligible for discharge. It didn't say it was automatic. If his commanding officer felt he needed him in his company, his decision was final; you could not appeal it to any higher position.

I applied, based upon the fact that I was eligible as I was thirty-eight before March 1, 1943. The application came back to me marked "Disapproved" and signed by my commanding officer. That seemed final, but there is nothing final in this world if you know who God is. If you know that your own Wonderful Human Imagination is God, you do not accept anything on the outside that is in conflict with your desires.

I desired to be honorably discharged and out of the army, but here was the discharge paper marked disapproved and signed by my commanding officer.

That night as I retired in my barracks with all these men around me, I assumed I was in my own apartment in New York City. I had left a wife and a little girl only a few months old when I was drafted. So, I imagined I was home. My wife is in that bed; I am in the bed and my little girl is over there in the crib. Then I simply assumed I am walking through the apartment from room to room. I touched some objects and they all seemed so familiar.

I looked through the window and saw Washington Square, then to the right and saw Sixth Avenue. Then I returned to my bed and settled in it. All these things I did in my imagination, but I gave it the tone of reality. I gave it sensory vividness. I made it so real that it seemed to me I am actually in my apartment in New York City. I made quite sure I was not there on furlough, I was there because I was honorably discharged.

At four o'clock in the morning, before my eyes came a sheet of paper like the sheet I had received from my Colonel where it was disapproved. As I looked at it, a hand appeared holding a pen and scratched out the word, "Disapproved," and wrote boldly in script, "Approved." Then the voice said to me, "That which I have done, I have done. Do nothing."

For nine days I did nothing, and then on the tenth day the same Colonel called me in, and after a long chat he said "Go back to your commanding officer and tell him to fill out another application." This I did. The Colonel approved it and that very day I was on a train to New York City, honorably discharged.

To this day, none of them knew what I did, for I did it all in my imagination and I believed that what I did was fact. I believed that my imaginal acts create facts and, therefore, I lived in my apartment as a civilian and not a soldier, because I was honorably discharged from the army—and in nine days it was fulfilled.

I could multiply that story by hundreds if one would actually do it, for we are the operant power. Instead of

doing strange things and getting in wrong with the government and fighting for your objectives, you don't fight at
all. The voice said to me, "That which I have done, I have
done. Do nothing."

Where was that voice? Within me. That very voice that
I heard coming from without was whispering from within
me. The voice that said to Moses, "I Am, that is who I
AM," he heard as coming from without, but it was whispered from within. For are we not told in scripture that we
are the temple of the living God, and the Spirit of God
dwells in us, then how can I hear it from another?

I ask everyone to believe in God, but God is not something on the outside of you; God is your own Wonderful
Human Imagination. If you have any other god, you have a
false god. Always exercise your imagination lovingly on
behalf of everyone in this world. It doesn't cost you anything and it doesn't hurt anyone. Then you will find yourself becoming the man you want to be, the lady you want
to be, without hurting anyone. You will fulfill all of your
dreams.

Then you will know how true the statement is that
"All things are possible to him who believes," because with
God all things are possible and you have found God. You
have found Him in yourself as your own wonderful human
imagination.

Scripture is the greatest book in the world. It teaches
you, tells you, invites and encourages you to exercise your
imagination lovingly on behalf of anything in this world.
You cannot fail in achieving your goal if you know who
you are.

No external god is going to help you. There is no external god. God actually, literally became man, that man
may become God. He isn't pretending He is man; He literally became man, and completely emptied Himself of His
divine power and took upon Himself the limitations and
restrictions of man. Finding Himself man, He is now subject to all the weaknesses of man. But, in the end, He

remembers who He is. Then, as man remembers who he is,
he shares that memory with his brothers. For, we are all
one. There is only one God, one God buried in this fragmented state called humanity.

If you know exactly what you want in this world and
are willing to assume you have it, sleep tonight as though it
were true. Make a mental image of friends round about
you congratulating you on your good fortune. See them in
that act; don't make any excuses about it; accept it as a
fact and it will be seen by the world.

The Catholic Bible translates this statement best of all
as far as I am concerned. It's the 17th verse of the 4th
chapter of Romans: they say, "God calls things that are
not seen as though they were, and the unseen becomes
seen." The Protestant Bibles, both the King James and the
Revised Standard Version say, "He calls into existence the
things that do not exist." That I question. To me all things
exist. All things exist in the human imagination but I need
not call them into being. I can select the one that I want to
call into being, but I cannot say I call into existence the
things that do not exist because they do exist. But they are
unseen by mortal eye, so I call it into being.

These unseen things are states of consciousness and all
states exist. They are with us now. You and I are travelers
and we travel through states as a pilgrim travels through
cities. He leaves the city behind but the city remains. So I
travel through states. I can travel through the state of
poverty. Poverty remains for anyone to enter it, but, having shared it for a while, I didn't like it, so I moved out of
the state called poverty but I don't destroy it. The state is
there for everyone to enter.

You can feel sorry for yourself and in no time flat you
will find yourself in a state you do not like. But you can't
see it as a state and you inquire, "What's wrong with me?"
You are only in a state. Don't condemn the man for the
state he is in; it's the state and you can't kill the state or
destroy it. The state is there as a permanent fixture of the
universe.

But, you can move him out of the state. Represent him to yourself as the man he would like to be and see him as that man in your own mind's eye. The state will remain for anyone, either willingly or unwillingly to enter. We are all moving through states. You find you can go wherever you want to. It's not the privilege of the rich; it's the privilege of the man who can imagine.

I had no power or pull to get myself out of the army. I didn't need wealth; I didn't need any social or financial background; all I needed was to remember that I AM HE. Are we not told in the 46th Psalm, "Be still and know that I am God." Man may say, "You can't be that arrogant." All right, if you aren't going to be that arrogant, remain where you are. It's perfectly all right; the state doesn't care how long you occupy it. You can occupy it from the cradle to the grave and it doesn't care, but, while you are in a state, you are going to illuminate and reap the fruit of it.

But, knowing they are states, select a more desirable one and enter it. How do I enter a state? It's all a mood. Did not Churchill tell us that the mood determines the fortunes of people rather than the fortunes determine the mood. He knew what he was talking about. The fortunes are not determining the mood; the mood determines the fortunes.

I will assume the feeling of the wish fulfilled. I believe it was Anthony Eden who told us that an assumption, though false, if persisted in, will harden into fact. Both of these men were Prime Ministers of England, and a third Prime Minister was Benjamin Disraeli, who said, "Man is not the victim of circumstances; circumstances are created by man." It's entirely up to me. I simply enter a state by a mood. I contemplate the desire. Then ask myself the question, "What would it be like if it were true?" If I dare to assume it is true, that's my way to success. The feeling of the wish fulfilled, sustained, is man's road to success.

Dream nobly and don't be limited by your present state, for that's only a state. You, the occupant of the

present state, are equal with every being in this world, for
there is only God and the occupant of any state is God.
One who has a billion today is in a state of fabulous
wealth, but he, the occupant, is the same being you are
and it's God. There is nothing but God.

The one who is enjoying great health and the one who
is not enjoying good health, they are still the same being.
Ask the simple question, "What would it be like . . ." and
then catch the mood. As you catch the mood, the fortune
follows. We are always believing ahead of our evidence.
Don't wait for evidence; you precede the evidence by your
belief and the belief is caught by a mood.

There isn't a thing in this world that was not first
imagined.

The clothes you wear, the very building in which we
are now housed had to first be imagined. All these preceded the evidence that came into the world. But if you go
beyond that and say, "Well, after all, the stones were not,
the trees were not." Yes they were. They were all imagined
in the depths of your own being and then came to the
surface in these garments.

You can see the evidence of what man has imagined.
He had to first imagine going to the moon before he could
conceive of the means to get there. You and I have to
imagine everything before it can become a fact in this
world, for there isn't a thing that you and I call a fact that
was not first imagined.

Objective reality is solely produced through imagining.
You can start now to imagine a more noble world for
yourself and for your immediate circle. If you imagine it
and believe that what you have imagined is fact, it will
become a fact, for I tell you imagining creates reality.
Because God, imagining, is creating and man, imagining, is
God, so he is creating.

Look at the world and see what we have done with it
because we did not know what we were doing. The morning's paper will show you the most horrible things in the

world and it's all man's imagination. It need not be, but we have fed it morning, noon and night because man has not controlled his imagination. Learn to control your own wonderful human imagination. When you do, you will have heaven on earth.

MENTAL
TRACKS

Have you lived your life in such a way you desire to live it again? If you haven't, start now, for may I tell you the next life is this life. Unless you awaken and change the tracks of this life, you will walk them forever. If you have not lived this life in such a way you desire to live it again, start now to interfere with these tracks and lay new ones.

Let me share a vision of mine with you. Lying on my bed the inner eye opened and I saw a man, casually dressed in working clothes, walking the sidewalk of a major city. As he came to a hole where coal had just been delivered, he dropped something from his hand, and, bending down, he picked up huge hunks of coal; then my vision relaxed.

When I reconcentrated my vision it was on the early part of the same scene and again I saw the man walking down the sidewalk. He came to the manhole, dropped something, and, bending down, he picked up a piece of coal as he had done before. Everything was in detail.

As I saw it the second time I said to myself, "That scene hasn't changed one iota." My attention again relaxed and when I reconcentrated it, it was on the early part of the scene. Now I could prophesy for that man; I knew exactly what he would do every moment of time right up to that manhole; he would drop his package and, not picking it up, he would pick up the coal. I knew he would look into the manhole and then change his mind, either because someone below saw him or he had a change of heart, but I knew in detail what that man would do.

We are walking tracks and the tracks are forever, and by the mere curvature of time your next life is this life. You simply replay it; so if you are not proud of it, start now and change your life today.

The system by which you change it is this. You are standing forever in the presence of an infinite and eternal energy. From this energy all things proceed, but they proceed according to a pattern. Energy is moving in a certain pattern and you determine the pattern it takes, for you lay down these tracks within you by the use of your inner conversations. This energy, I call mind, follows the tracks laid down in a man's own inner talking.

If your inner conversations are not what they should be, change them. Start carrying on conversations within yourself from premises of fulfilled ideals. If you are not now the man, the woman you want to be, begin to assume you are and inwardly carry on conversations with your friends. Have them see you as the man, the woman you want them to see. These inner words are really the breeding ground of future action. They will lay down new tracks and then the energy which is always flowing will flow over these tracks, and the conditions and circumstances of your life will change. If you do not lay new tracks, I will prophesy for you, you will find yourself repeating the same life over and over again, but you will do it so automatically you will not know you have done it before.

If I could take you into the inner vision with me you would see this room rising. Everything rising in detail like a three dimensional curtain ascending, yet it remains. Every moment of time the whole is ascending, yet it remains the same. It's almost as though not a thing has happened. But if the inner eye opens you see it ascend, rising in a three dimensional manner; so when a man goes over these tracks he is totally unaware he has walked them before.

I bring you this message to make you conscious. Man

must awake from the dream where he is simply an automa-
ton, moving like a machine. When he awakes he is not the
man he seemed to be; he awakes a new being, a new man.

The new man is a man of new conversations. We are
told in Ephesians, "Put off the former conversations; they
belong to the old man that is corrupt, and put on the new
man by a transformation of your mind."

The new man is identified with new words. He speaks
only kind words. He is incapable of any unlovely thought;
incapable of even listening to the unlovely. When you do
this you find yourself awakening the Lord Jesus Christ,
who is your own wonderful human imagination. Every
time you use your imagination lovingly on behalf of
another you are literally awakening this inner man and
mediating God to man. If I think of anyone in a loving
way, I am in contact with that being and God flows
toward him.

Imagine yourself at the base of a wonderful waterfall;
the water is flowing on you and through you. Now see it
flowing from you towards someone else. I make this statement because it's a true statement; we are now in Eden but
we are asleep. Do you want to awaken? Do this:

Just imagine yourself the center through which water
radiates, and every one in this world is rooted in you and
ends in you, as I AM rooted in God and end in God. You
are in God's garden, it's Eden, and every man in the world
has a plot in the garden.

Let me now look at my friend's plot in my garden. As
I look I see trees, some called health, others wealth. I see a
tree of dignity, one of nobility and even a tree of being
wanted. They may be withered because they are in need of
water, so I water them, and in my mind's eye I watch the
leaves appear on that which was formerly a barren plant. I
see the fruit appear and I know, wherever my friend is in
this world, as I water his garden (which is really my own
garden) he will embody the very qualities the tree is now
beginning to bear and radiate.

You name the tree. Your friend feels unwanted? You

name it and let the water flow towards it. See it growing healthy in that garden. See it put out leaves and bring forth fruit. And wherever he is he will begin to be wanted by people in his world. If he is unemployed, it's a tree of employment. See it radiate its leaves and its fruit and he will be gainfully employed.

This is not just an idle statement; everyone can and should do it. Whenever you water a tree in the garden of another you are watering your own garden in the eternal one of God. For every man can make this statement: "I am the vine and ye are the branches."

You, individually, are the central vine of God's garden and everyone in your world is a branch of that vine. When I, as a central vine, water a branch in my garden, at that same moment I am being watered. I don't have to water my own, just be taking care of the many gardens in God's Eden. I take care of my own garden which is in the vine of everyone in the world.

Try it and bless everyone in the world. Eventually the eye opens, the ear opens and the inner man awakes. Then you will see the most glorious world which has always been there, but we, in our sleep, have shut it out.

Take me seriously, for your next life is this life. Make this life what you want it to be, because if you don't you will find yourself automatically walking the same track repeating this life. If I could only take you within me and let you see with the inner eye, you would see everyone in the world as automatons, just sleeping people. Yes, their eye is open and they seem to be awake, but they are really sound asleep, for they're repeating the same things.

"Awake, O sleeper from the land of dreams." When you awake you enter the conscious circle of humanity, or as my old teacher used to call it, "The Brothers." When you awake you are a glorious being, for you are the image of the Divine One.

Start today, start learning the art of revision. At the end of this day review it. If some unlovely thing happened, rewrite it. Having rewritten it, replay it. As you replay it you've changed it. That moment never receded into the past, but always advances into the future to confront you.

Yesterday is today's future. You may think it's past, but, by the curvature of time, you will discover it is not. When you begin to awaken you will come upon yesteryear in your future, and if you don't change it you will simply find yourself repeating it over and over, thinking you are doing it for the first time. But I ask you to awake that we may all enter this brotherhood of awakened humanity.

We are told there were two gifts given to man at birth. It doesn't mean this little birth when I left my mother's womb, but when I left the womb of my Father, the grand womb, the womb of creation. Before the world was, He created me and make me perfect. He sent me into this world for a purpose, an educative purpose. But He gave me two gifts; He gave me His mind, and He gave me the gift of speech, the very thing He used to create a world.

If I use the gift wisely I will be led into the fulfillment of my every desire. If I continually use it wisely, when I quit the body and the world calls me dead, I go into another dimension by the wise use of the same two gifts. If I awake I will break the circle of recurrence and rise beyond it into eternity, into the company of the blessed. But if I don't use it wisely, I continue my circle of sleep on the curved line of time and repeat it over and over until one day I awake, for I am destined to be conformed to the image of His son.

I have no doubt everyone will awake, but why not start the awakening process now? Start by practicing the art of revision. Try it with your friends, remembering you are the grand waterfall.

The word water in scripture means truth. When I see anyone in my mind's eye and see him free, I am giving him the only truth that can set him free. If I water his plant, imagining the water is really going to it, I see the leaves begin to appear and that man becoming free, healthy, secure and loved. Then I know those trees are growing beautifully in my garden. As I do that, not only will he benefit from my watering his plant, but I will benefit, for I will begin to awaken.

I ask everyone to try it. If you wait, thinking there is going to be some change beyond the grave. All transforming power is *in* man *now* to interfere with his time track. You interfere with it by simply changing one moment in the course of a day. Go back to that moment in time, revise it, replay it in the revised version and do it over and over in your imagination until it takes on the tones of reality. As it takes on the tones of reality you have changed your future. Take another incident and change it. Keep on changing all the little episodes, all the little experiences, and make them conform to a more idealistic experience; then relive it.

Try it, and when the inner man awakens you will see a world that is automatic like a machine. You will see everyone playing the parts they've played forever and will continue to play on the curvature of time, until He awakes and rises from the dead. You are told, "Awake thou that sleepest and rise from the dead."

The state called sleep is likened unto death. We are told the second son, the prodigal son, returned to his father who said: "He that was lost is found, and he that was dead is alive again." The purpose now is to rise. Not to amass a fortune, although you are entitled to it. Not to become famous, although you are entitled to that, but simply to awake from the state of sleep, and I know of no other way to awaken man unless I show him how mechanical he is.

I ask everyone to take me seriously. If this seems a bit too mystical for you, I don't apologize; it's the only thing I can give, for as I begin to awake I've got to give you the food on which my Father feeds me. He feeds me new ideas; He changes my values, He changes all the meanings in my world. Nothing has the same meaning it had last year. My values have changed. I can't place it on wealth, on names or on recognition. As you awaken all your values change and then you begin to inwardly see a new wonderful world.

This world we live in is the garden of which I speak and it is a true garden. This wonderful visible objective world of ours is not a place of exile, it's the living garment of our Father. Everything in your world is related, by affinity, to your own mental activity.

If you were conscious of the activity within you, you would see everything related to your imagination. That activity, could you see it, projects the conditions and circumstances of your life. Not one thing is out of order. Change the activity and you change the world in which you live. You change that activity by changing your inner speech, for speech mirrors your mind and your mind mirrors God. If you don't change the activity you can't change the conditions of life, for they only come bearing witness of this inner action of your mind.

If, right now you reflect upon your life and say within yourself, "I wouldn't want to live this again," then you'd better start changing it, because I can make you a promise, your next life is this life. If you cannot, now, in reflection, say, "I desire to live it again," then start today to lay down new tracks, for you stand in the presence of energy and you can't stop walking. The curvature of time will bring you back and back and back, forever and forever, until you break it. Then you awaken and enter a circle of awakened humanity. I'll tell you, you know them more intimately than anyone you now know in the state of sleep. There is not a person on earth that you know as intimately as those who have awakened when you awake. When you go into their presence you mingle and become one with them. You do not lose your identity; in fact, you tend ever toward greater and greater individualization. You never become absorbed and lose your identity, but as you awaken you awaken to the being you always were but had forgotten when you fell asleep. There is a beauty in the inner man that the outer has never touched, never scarred, and as you awaken they will be

there to meet you, because they are eagerly awaiting the
breaking of the circle of recurrence.

I give you the end of a golden string and call upon you
to roll it into a ball. If you do it will lead you in at
heaven's gate built in Jerusalem's wall. I cannot do it for
you, but call upon you to wind it and roll it into a ball by
the daily application of the principle of revision, by daily
watching your inner actions, and see if they correspond to
the actions you desire to perform in the outer world.

Watch your conversations carefully; are they from
premises of fulfilled desires? If they are not, go back and
make them correspond to the ideal you want to embody in
this world.

Start revising this day and watch the circle begin to
snap, watch the eye begin to open. I tell you when the eye
opens there isn't a possession in the world that you would
want more than the opening of that eye. Your values
change, the meaning of life changes, for you wouldn't sell
the eye that opens for all the wealth of the world. You
wouldn't exchange it for any recognition in the world now
conferred upon the so-called great. You see the so-called
great all equally sound asleep playing their parts walking
curved lines. But you have snapped it, and move into a
wonderful world of awakened humanity, and there you see
these glorified beings, but really glorified beings, who preceded you into the conscious circle of humanity.